Level 4

Retold by John and Celia Turvey
Series Editors: Andy Hopkins and Jocelyn Potter

Pearson Education Limited
Edinburgh Gate, Harlow,
Essex CM20 2JE, England
and Associated Companies throughout the world.

ISBN 0 582 419190

This compilation first published in Longman Fiction 1998
This edition first published 1999

NEW EDITION

5 7 9 10 8 6 4

The story "Three is a Lucky Number" © Margery Allingham is reproduced by
permission of Curtis Brown, London on behalf of P. & M. Youngman Carter Ltd.
The story "Full Circle"by Sue Grafton is reprinted with the permission of Abner
Stein, London. The story "How's Your Mother?" © Simon Brett 1980 is from *A Box of
Tricks*, published by Victor Gollancz Ltd. The story "At the Old Swimming Hole"
© 1986 Sara Paretsky was first published in *Mean Streets: The Second Private Eye
Writers of America Anthology*, edited by Robert J. Randisi, published by Mysterious
Press. All rights reserved. First published in the UK by Hamish Hamilton Limited.
The Patricia Highsmith story "Slowly, Slowly in the Wind" was first published in
Ellery Queen's Mystery Magazine 1976. Copyright © 1993 Diogenes Verlag AG,
Zurich. The Patricia Highsmith story "Woodrow Wilson's Neck Tie" was first
published in *Ellery Queen's Mystery Magazine 1972*. Copyright © 1993 Diogenes
Verlag AG, Zurich. The story "The Absence of Emily" by Jack Ritchie is reprinted
with kind permission of the Larry Sternig & Jack Byrne Literary Agency, Milwaukee,
United States of America. The story "The Inside Story" © 1993 Colin Dexter. This
abridgement and simplification © Addison Wesley Longman Limited 1997.

This edition copyright © Penguin Books Ltd 1999
Ilustrations by Les Edwards
Cover design by Bender Richardson White

Set in 11/14pt Bembo
Printed in Spain by Mateu Cromo, S.A. Pinto (Madrid)

Published by Pearson Education Limited in association with
Penguin Books Ltd, both companies being subsidiaries of Pearson Plc

For a complete list of titles available in the Penguin Readers series please write to your local
Pearson Education office or contact: Penguin Readers Marketing Department,
Pearson Education, Edinburgh Gate, Harlow, Essex, CM20 2JE.

Contents

Introduction

This collection contains eight murder stories written by some of the finest British and American mystery writers of the twentieth century. Many, like Colin Dexter and Patricia Highsmith, are best known for their full-length works while others, like Jack Ritchie, specialize in the short story. In some of these stories, like Sara Paretsky's 'At the Old Swimming Hole', we follow the action through the eyes of the person who is trying to solve the crime. Other stories are told from the point of view of the criminal; as readers of Patricia Highsmith's 'Woodrow Wilson's Tie', we share the murderer's thoughts as well as his actions.

English mystery writer Margery Allingham (1904–66) was born in London. She followed other members of her family into a life of writing, producing her first mystery story in 1927. She also wrote about social history. In 'Three Is a Lucky Number' we meet Ronald Torbay, who is making careful preparations for his third murder. But will he succeed?

Born in Kentucky in 1940, Sue Grafton, who now lives in California, has won many prizes for her crime stories. Kinsey Millhone, a strong, intelligent female private detective with a good sense of humour, is the main character in her books and short stories. 'Full Circle' takes place in the imaginary town of Santa Teresa in California. It seems that there has been a terrible car accident. But was it really an accident?

British crime writer Simon Brett was born in 1945. After studying at Oxford University, he worked as a producer for BBC radio and London Weekend Television. He has written a number of radio and TV plays in addition to his books and short stories. Humphrey Partridge, the main character in 'How's Your Mother?', lives alone with his sick mother. But nobody ever sees her, and when the house burns down she cannot be found. Where has she gone?

Sara Paretsky, born in Iowa in 1947, did a variety of jobs after leaving university before becoming a full-time writer. She has won many prizes for her crime writing and is particularly well known for her stories about V. I. Warshawski, a female private detective. In 'At the Old Swimming Hole', a woman is shot. V. I. follows the clues, but who is actually following who?

Patricia Highsmith (1921–95), who also wrote under the name Claire Morgan, was from Texas, although she lived in Europe for much of her later life. Her first book, *Strangers on a Train* (1950), was very successful and was made into a film by Alfred Hitchcock. She too won many writing prizes and two of her stories are included in this collection. 'Slowly, Slowly in the Wind' tells the story of an argument between neighbours that gets out of control. In 'Woodrow Wilson's Tie' a young delivery boy visits the waxworks and has a strange idea, but who will believe him?

American short story writer John George Reitci (1922–83) wrote under the name of Jack Ritchie. He was educated in Wisconsin, served in the United States Army, and wrote his best stories in the 1960s and 1970s. These stories have been reprinted many times in collections. A number of unusual detectives appear in his mystery stories; often they are not very good at detective work, and find the right solution by accident. In 'The Absence of Emily', Jack and Emily live next door to Emily's sister, Millicent. When Emily goes away without telling her, Millicent starts to worry. Is it possible that Jack has killed her?

Colin Dexter, born in 1930 in Lincolnshire, England, became a schoolteacher after leaving Cambridge University. He later moved to Oxford where many of his stories, including the Inspector Morse mysteries, take place. Morse works closely with

Sergeant Lewis, and the relationship between these two very different men develops with each story. In 'The Inside Story', a woman has been murdered. Clues include picture postcards and a crime story written by the dead woman. So who killed her? And why?

Three Is a Lucky Number *Margery Allingham*

At five o'clock on a September afternoon Ronald Torbay was
making preparations for his third murder. He was being very
careful. He realized that murdering people becomes more
dangerous if you do it often.

He was in the bathroom of the house that he had recently
rented. For a moment he paused to look in the mirror. The face
that looked back at him was thin, middle-aged and pale. Dark
hair, a high forehead and well-shaped blue eyes. Only the mouth
was unusual – narrow and quite straight. Even Ronald Torbay did
not like his own mouth.

A sound in the kitchen below worried him. Was Edyth
coming up to have her bath before he had prepared it for her?
No, it was all right: she was going out of the back door. From the
window he saw her disappearing round the side of the house
into the small square garden. It was exactly like all the other
gardens in the long street. She didn't like her to be alone there.
She was a shy person, but now new people had moved into the
house next door, and there was a danger of some silly woman
making friends with her. He didn't want that just now.

◆

Each of his three marriages had followed the same pattern. Using
a false name, he had gone on holiday to a place where no one
knew him. There he had found a middle-aged, unattractive
woman, with some money of her own and no family. He had
talked her into marrying him, and she had then agreed to make a
will which left him all her money. Both his other wives had been
shy, too. He was very careful to choose the right type of woman:
someone who would not make friends quickly in a new place.

1

Mary, the first of them, had had her deadly 'accident' almost unnoticed, in the bathroom of the house he had rented – a house very like this one, but in the north of England instead of the south. The police had not found anything wrong. The only person who was interested was a young reporter on the local newspaper. He had written something about death in the middle of happiness, and had printed photographs of Mary's wedding and her funeral, which took place only three weeks after the wedding.

Dorothy had given him a little more trouble. It was not true that she was completely alone in the world, as she had told him. Her brother had appeared at the funeral, and asked difficult questions about her money. There had been a court case, but Ronald had won it, and the insurance company had paid him the money.

All that was four years ago. Now, with a new name, a newly invented background, and a different area to work in, he felt quite safe.

From the moment he saw Edyth, sitting alone at a little table in the restaurant of a seaside hotel, he knew she was his next 'subject'. He could see from her face that she was not happy. And he could also see that she was wearing a valuable ring.

After dinner he spoke to her. She did not want to talk at first, but in the end he managed to start a conversation. After that, everything went as he expected. His methods were old-fashioned and romantic, and by the end of a week she was in love with him.

Her background was very suitable for Ronald's purpose. After teaching at a girls' school for ten years, she had gone home to look after her sick father and had stayed with him until he died. Now, aged forty-three, she was alone, with a lot of money, and she didn't know what to do with herself.

Five weeks after they met, Ronald married her, in the town where they were both strangers. The same afternoon they both made a will leaving all their property to each other. Then they moved into the house which he had rented cheaply because the holiday season was at an end. It was the most pleasant of his marriages. He found Edyth a cheerful person, and even quite sensible – except that it was stupid of her to believe that a man would fall in love with her at first sight. Ronald knew he must not make the mistake of feeling sorry for her. He began to make plans for 'her future', as he called it.

Two things made him do this earlier than he intended. One was the way she refused to talk about her money. She kept all her business papers locked in a desk drawer, and refused to discuss them. His other worry was her unnecessary interest in his job. Ronald had told Edyth that he was a partner in an engineering company, which was giving him a long period of absence. Edyth accepted the story, but she asked a lot of questions and wanted to visit his office and the factory.

So Ronald had decided that it was time to act.

He turned from the window, and began to run water into the bath. His heart was beating loudly, he noticed. He didn't like that. He needed to keep very calm.

The bathroom was the only room they had painted. He had done it himself soon after they arrived. He had also put up the little shelf over the bath which held their bottles and creams and a small electric heater. It was a cheap one, with two bars, and it was white, like the walls, and not too noticeable. There was no electric point in the bathroom, but he was able to connect the heater to a point just outside the door.

He turned on the heater now, and watched the bars become red and hot. Then he went out of the room. The controls for all the electricity in the house were inside a cupboard at the top of the stairs. Ronald opened the door carefully and pulled up the handle which turned off the electricity. (He had a cloth over his hand, so that he would not leave fingerprints.)

3

Back in the bathroom the bars of the heater were turning black again. Still using the cloth, he lifted the heater from the shelf and put it into the bath water, at the bottom end of the bath. Of course, you could still see it. It looked as if it had fallen off the shelf by accident.

Edyth was coming back from the garden: he could hear her moving something outside the kitchen door. He pulled a small plastic bottle out of his pocket and began to read again the directions on the back.

A small sound behind him made him turn suddenly. There was Edyth's head, only two metres away, appearing above the flat roof of the kitchen which was below the bathroom window. She was clearing the dead leaves from the edge of the roof. She must be standing on the ladder which was kept outside the kitchen door.

He stayed calm. 'What are you doing there, dear?'

Edyth was so surprised that she nearly fell off the ladder. 'Oh, you frightened me! I thought I'd just do this little job before I came to get ready.'

'But I'm preparing your beauty bath for you.'

'It's kind of you to take all this trouble, Ronald.'

'Not at all. I'm taking you out tonight and I want you to look as nice as − er − possible. Hurry up, dear. The bubbles don't last very long, and like all these beauty treatments, this one's expensive. Go and undress now, and come straight here.'

'Very well, dear.' She began to climb down the ladder.

Ronald opened the little bottle, and poured the liquid into the bath. He turned on the water again, and in a moment the bath was full of bubbles, smelling strongly of roses. They covered the little heater completely; they even covered the sides of the bath.

Edyth was at the door. 'Oh Ronald! It's all over everything − even on the floor!'

'That doesn't matter. You get in quickly, before it loses its strength. I'll go and change now. Get straight in and lie down. It

4

He turned on the water again . . .

will give your skin a bit of colour!'

He went out and paused, listening. She locked the door, as he expected. He walked slowly to the electricity box, and forced himself to wait another minute.

'How is it?' he shouted.

'I don't know yet. I've only just got into the bath. It smells nice.'

His hand, covered with the cloth, was on the controls.

'One, two . . . three,' he said, and pulled the handle down. A small explosion from the electric point behind him told him that the electricity had gone off. Then everything was silent.

After a time he went and knocked on the bathroom door.

'Edyth?'

There was no answer, no sound, nothing.

Now he had to prepare the second stage. As he knew well, this was the difficult bit. The discovery of the body must be made, but not too soon. He had made that mistake with Dorothy's 'accident', and the police had asked him why he had got worried so soon. This time he decided to wait half an hour before he began to knock loudly on the bathroom door, then to shout for a neighbour and finally to force the lock.

There was something he wanted to do now. Edyth's leather writing-case, which contained all her private papers, was in the drawer where she kept her blouses. He had discovered it some time ago, but he had not forced the lock open because that would frighten her. Now there was nothing to stop him.

He went softly into the bedroom and opened the drawer. The case was there. The lock was more difficult than he expected, but he finally managed to open the case. Inside there were some financial documents, one or two thick envelopes and, on top of these, her Post Office Savings book.

He opened it with shaking fingers, and began reading the figures – £17,000 . . . £18,600 . . . £21,940 . . . He turned over a page, and his heart jumped wildly. On 4th September she had taken almost all the money out of her savings account!

Perhaps it was here, in these thick envelopes? He opened one of them; papers, letters, documents fell on the floor.

Suddenly he saw an envelope with his own name on it, in Edyth's writing. He pulled it open, and saw in surprise that the date on the letter was only two days ago.

Dear Ronald,

If you ever read this, I am afraid it will be a terrible shock to you. I hoped it would not be necessary to write it, but now your behaviour has forced me to face some very unpleasant possibilities.

Did you not realize, Ronald, that any middle-aged woman who has been rushed into marriage to a stranger will ask herself about her husband's reason for marrying her?

At first I thought I was in love with you, but when you asked me to make my will on our wedding day, I began to worry. And then, when you started making changes to the bathroom in this house, I decided to act quickly. So I went to the police.

Have you noticed that the people who have moved into the house next door have never spoken to you? Well, they are not a husband and wife, but a police inspector and a policewoman. The policewoman showed me two pieces from old newspapers, both about women who had died from accidents in their baths soon after their marriages. Both pieces included a photograph of the husband at the funeral. They were not very clear, but I was able to recognize you. So I realized that it was my duty to agree to do what the Inspector asked me to do. (The police have been looking for the man since the photographs were given to them by your second wife's brother.) The Inspector said the police needed to be sure that you were guilty: you must be given the opportunity to try the crime again. That's why I am forcing myself to be brave, and to play my part.

I want to tell you something, Ronald. If one day you lose me, out of the bathroom, I mean, you will find that I have gone out over the kitchen roof, and am sitting in the kitchen next door. I was stupid to marry you, but not quite as stupid as you thought.

Yours,

EDYTH.

Ronald's mouth was uglier than ever when he finished reading the letter. The house was still quiet. But in the silence he heard the back door open suddenly, and heavy footsteps rushed up the stairs towards him.

Full Circle   *Sue Grafton*

The accident happened on a Friday afternoon, as I was driving home. The traffic was moving quickly along the Santa Teresa freeway and my own little Volkswagen was running well, although it's fifteen years old. I was feeling good. I'd just solved a difficult case, and I had a cheque in my handbag for four thousand dollars. That's good money, for a female private detective working for herself.

The sun shone down on the freeway out of a cloudless California sky. I was driving in the middle lane. Looking into the driving mirror, I saw a young woman in a small white car coming up behind me in the fast lane. A bright red Porsche was close behind her, and I guessed she wanted to move into the middle lane in front of me to let it pass, so I reduced my speed. Coming up on my right was a dark blue Toyota. While I was looking in the mirror I heard a loud noise, a bit like a gunshot.

I turned my attention back to the road in front of me. Suddenly the small white car moved back into the fast lane. It seemed to be out of control. It hit the back of the red Porsche, ran into the fence in the centre of the freeway, and then back again into the road in front of me. I put my foot down hard to bring the Volkswagen to a stop. At that moment a green Mercedes suddenly appeared from nowhere, and hit the side of the girl's car, sending it right off the road. Behind me all the cars were trying to stop – I could hear them crashing into each other.

It was all over in a moment. A cloud of dust from the side of the road showed where the girl's car had come to rest. It had hit one of the posts of a road sign, and the broken sign was now hanging across her car roof.

I left my car at the side of the road and ran towards the white car, with the man from the blue Toyota close behind me. The girl's head had gone through the front window. She was unconscious, and her face was covered in blood. I couldn't open the car door, but the man from the Toyota forced it open and reached inside.

'Don't move her,' I said. 'Let the ambulance people do it.' I took off my coat, and we used it to stop the blood from the worst of her cuts. He was a man of twenty-four or twenty-five, with dark hair and anxious dark eyes.

Someone behind me was asking for help, and I realized that other people had been hurt in the accident as well. The driver from the green Mercedes was already using the telephone at the roadside, to call the ambulance and police, I guessed. The driver of the red Porsche just stood there, unable to move from shock. I looked back at the young man from the Toyota, who was pressing the girl's neck. 'She seems to be alive,' he said.

I left him with the girl, and went to help a man with a broken leg.

By the time the police and the ambulance arrived, a small crowd of drivers had stopped their cars to look, as if a road accident was some kind of sports event. I noticed my friend John Birkett, a photographer from the local newspaper. I watched as the girl was carried into the ambulance. Then, with some of the other drivers, I had to tell a policeman what I had seen.

When I read in the newspaper next morning that the girl had died, I was so upset that I felt sick. There was a short piece about her. Caroline Spurrier was twenty-two, a student in her final year at the University of California, Santa Teresa. She came from Denver, Colorado. The photograph showed shoulder-length fair hair, bright eyes and a happy smile. I could feel the young woman's death like a heavy weight on my chest.

My office in town was being painted, so I worked at home that next week. On Thursday morning there was a knock at the

'Don't move her.'

door. I opened it. At first I thought the dead girl was alive again, and standing on my doorstep. But then I realized that this was a woman in her forties.

'I'm Michelle Spurrier,' she said. 'I understand you saw my daughter's accident.'

'Please come in. I'm so sorry about what happened.'

She couldn't speak at first, then the words came slowly. 'The police examined Caroline's car, and found a bullet hole in the window on the passenger side. My daughter was shot.' She began to cry. When she was calmer I asked, 'What do the police say about it?'

'They're calling it murder now. The officer I talked to thinks it's one of those freeway killings – a crazy man shooting at a passing car, for no special reason.'

'They've had enough of those in Los Angeles,' I said.

'Well, I can't accept that. Why was she on the freeway instead of at work? She had a job in the afternoons. They tell me she left suddenly without a word to anyone.'

'Where did she work?'

'At a restaurant near the university. She'd been working there for a year. The manager told me a man had been annoying her. Perhaps she left to get away from him.'

'Did he know who the man was?'

'Not really. They had been out together. He kept coming to see her in the restaurant, calling her at all hours, causing a lot of trouble. Lieutenant Dolan tells me you're a private detective – I want you to find out who's responsible for her death.'

'Mrs Spurrier, the police here are very good at their job. I'm sure they're doing everything possible.'

'I'm not so sure. But I have to fly back to Denver now. My husband is very ill and I need to get home. I can't go until I know someone here is looking into this. Please.'

I said I would do it. After all, I already had a strong interest in the case. 'I'll need a few names,' I said.

She gave me the names of the girl who shared Caroline's room and the restaurant where she'd worked.

Usually I try to keep out of cases that the police are working on. Lieutenant Dolan, the officer responsible for murder cases, is not fond of private detectives. So I was surprised that he'd sent Mrs Spurrier to me.

As soon as she left, I drove over to the police station, where I paid six dollars for a copy of the police report. Lieutenant Dolan wasn't in, so I spoke to Emerald, the secretary who works in the Records Department.

'I'd like a bit of information on the Spurrier accident. Did anybody see where the shot was fired from?'

'No, they didn't.'

I thought about the man in the red Porsche. He'd been in the lane to my left, just a few metres ahead of me when the accident happened. The man in the Toyota might be a help as well. 'What about the other witnesses? There were five or six of us there. Who's been questioned?'

Emerald looked angry. 'You know I'm not allowed to give out information like that!'

'Come on, Emerald. Dolan knows I'm doing this. He told Mrs Spurrier about me. Just give me one name.'

'Well . . . Which one?' Slowly she got out some papers.

I described the young man in the Toyota, thinking she could find him in the list of witnesses by his age.

She looked down the list. 'Uh-oh! The man in the Toyota gave a false name and address. Benny Seco was the name, but I guess he invented that. Perhaps he's already wanted by the police.'

I heard a voice behind me. 'Well, well. Kinsey Millhone. Hard at work, I see.'

I turned to find Lieutenant Dolan standing there, his hands in his pockets. I smiled brightly. 'Mrs Spurrier got in touch with me and asked me to find out more about her daughter's death. I feel bad about the girl. What's the story on the missing witness?'

'I'm sure he had a reason for giving a false name,' said Dolan. 'Did you talk to him yourself?'

'Just for a few moments, but I'd know him if I saw him again. Do you think he could help us?'

'I'd certainly like to hear what he has to say. The other witnesses didn't realize that the girl was shot. I understand he was close enough to do it himself.'

'There must be a way to find him, don't you think?'

'No one remembers much about the man except the car he drove. Toyota, dark blue, four or five years old.'

'Would you mind if I talked to the other witnesses? I might get more out of them because I was there.'

He looked at me for a moment, and then gave me the list.

'Thanks. This is great. I'll tell you what I find out.'

I drove to the restaurant where Caroline Spurrier had worked. I introduced myself to the manager, and told him I was looking into Caroline's death.

'Oh, yes, that was terrible. I talked to her mother.'

'She told me you said something about a man who was annoying Caroline. What else can you tell me?'

'That's about all I know. I never saw the man myself. She was working nights for the last two months. She just went back to working days to try to get away from him.'

'Did she ever tell you his name?'

'Terry, I think. She really thought he was crazy.'

'Why did she go out with him?'

'She said he seemed really nice at first, but then he got very jealous. He used to follow her around all the time, in a green Ford car. In the end, I guess he was completely crazy. He probably came to find her at the restaurant on Friday afternoon, and that's why she left.'

I thanked him, and drove over to the university houses where Caroline had lived.

The girl who had shared her room was busy packing things in boxes. Her name was Judy Layton. She was twenty-two, a History student whose family lived in the town. When I asked why she didn't live at home, she explained that she had a difficult relationship with her mother.

'How long did you know Caroline?'

'About a year. I didn't know her well.'

I looked at the boxes. 'So you're moving out?'

'I'm going back to my parents' house. It's near the end of the school year now. And my parents are away for a month, in Canada. My brother's coming to help me move.'

'Did Caroline have a boyfriend?'

'She went out with lots of boys.'

'But no one special?'

She shook her head, not looking at me.

I tried again. 'She told her mother about a man who annoyed her at work. They'd been going out together. They'd just finished a relationship. I expect she told you about him?'

'No, she didn't. She and I were not close. She went her way and I went mine.'

'Judy, people get murdered for a reason. There was something going on. Can't you help me?'

'You don't know it was murder. The policeman I talked to said perhaps it was a crazy man in a passing car.'

'Her mother doesn't agree.'

'Well, I can't help. I've told you everything I know.'

I spent the next two days talking to Caroline's teachers and friends. She seemed to be a sweet girl, well-liked by everyone. But I didn't get any useful information. I went back to the list of witnesses to the accident, talking to each in turn. I was still interested in the man with the Toyota. What reason could he have

'What's this about?'

for giving a false name? I didn't seem to be making any progress. Then an idea came to me as I was looking at the newspaper picture of the crashed car. I suddenly remembered John Birkett at the scene of the crash, taking pictures. Perhaps he had one of the man in the Toyota? Twenty minutes later I was in Birkett's office at the *Santa Teresa News*, looking at the photographs.

'No good,' John said. 'No clear pictures of him.'

'What about his car?'

John pulled out another photo of Caroline's car, with the Toyota some distance behind.

'Can you make it bigger?'

'Are you looking for anything special?'

'The numberplate,' I said.

When we had made the photograph bigger we were able to read the seven numbers and letters on the California numberplate. I knew I should inform Lieutenant Dolan, but I wanted to work on this myself. So I telephoned a friend of mine at the Department of Motor Vehicles.

The number belonged to a 1984 Toyota, dark blue, and the owner was Ron Cagle, with an address on McClatchy Way.

My heart was beating loudly as I rang the bell of the house. When the door was finally opened, I just stood there with my mouth open. Wrong man. This man was tall and fat, with blue eyes and red hair. 'Yes?' he said.

'I'm looking for Ron Cagle.'

'I'm Ron Cagle.'

'You are? You're the owner of a dark blue Toyota?' I read out the number of the car.

He gave me a strange look. 'Yes. Is something wrong?'

'Well, I don't know. Has someone else been driving it?'

'Not for the last six months. See for yourself.' He led me round the side of the house. There sat a dark blue Toyota, without wheels and without an engine. 'What's this about?' he asked.

'This car was at the scene of a recent accident where a girl was killed.'

'Not this one,' he said. 'This has been right here, in this condition, for six months.' He looked at it again in sudden surprise. 'What's this?' He pointed to the numberplate, and I saw that it had completely different numbers.

After a moment I realized what had happened. 'Somebody stole your plates, and put these in their place.'

'Why would they do that?'

'Perhaps they stole a Toyota like this, and wanted new numberplates for it, so the police wouldn't catch them.' You could see Cagle's car from the road, I noticed.

I called Lieutenant Dolan and told him what I'd found. He checked the list of stolen cars, and found that the number which was now on Cagle's car belonged to a vehicle reported stolen two weeks before. But Dolan thought that even if we found the man, he might not be connected with the shooting. I didn't believe him. I had to find that young man with the dark hair and the dark eyes.

◆

I looked through the list of witnesses and called everybody on the list. Most tried to be helpful, but there was nothing new to add. I drove back to the university area to look for Judy Layton. She must know something more.

The apartment was locked, and looking through the window I saw that all the furniture was gone. I spoke to the manager of the apartments and got the address of her parents' house in Colgate, the area to the north of town.

It was a pleasant house in a nice street. I rang the bell and waited. I rang the bell again. It appeared that no one was at home. As I was returning to my car, I noticed the three-car garage at the side of the house. In the detective business,

18

sometimes you get a feeling . . . a little voice inside you, telling you there's something wrong. I looked through the garage window. Inside I saw a car, with all the paint taken off it.

The side door of the garage was unlocked, and I went in. Yes, the car was a Toyota, and its numberplates were missing. This must be the same car – and the driver must be someone in the Layton family. But why hadn't he driven it away somewhere and left it? Perhaps he thought it was too dangerous? I did a quick search of the inside of the car. Under the front seat I saw a handgun, a .45. I left it where it was, and ran back to my car. I had to find a telephone and call the police.

As I was getting into my car, I saw a dark green Ford coming towards the Layton entrance. The driver was the man I'd seen at the accident. Judy's brother? He looked rather like her. Of course she hadn't wanted to talk about him!

Suddenly he noticed me, and I saw the terror in his face as he recognized me. The Ford sped past me, and I chased after it. I guessed he was going towards the freeway.

He wasn't far in front of me when he turned onto the freeway, heading south, and soon I was right behind him.

He turned off the road onto the rough ground beside it, to pass the slow-moving traffic. I followed him. He was watching me in his driving mirror. Perhaps that was why he didn't see the workmen and their heavy vehicle right in front of him – not until it was too late.

He ran straight into the vehicle, with a crash that made my blood turn cold, as I brought the Volkswagen to a safe stop. It was like the first accident all over again, with police and ambulance men everywhere. Now I realized where I was. The workmen in their orange coats were putting up a new green freeway sign in place of the one that Caroline's car had broken. Terry Layton died at the exact spot where he had killed her.

But why did he do it? I guess the restaurant manager was

right, and jealousy had made him crazy. Not too crazy, though, to carry out that careful plan with the stolen car and numberplates. And now *he* was dead.

How's Your Mother?   *Simon Brett*

'It's all right, Mother. Just the post,' Humphrey Partridge called from the bottom of the stairs, as he opened the door to the village postman.

'There's a package for you, Mr Partridge,' said Reg Carter, putting his hand on the door. 'From a garden centre, it says on it. Roses, I think.'

'Yes,' said Partridge, trying to close the door.

'It's the right time of year for planting roses, is it? November?'

'Yes.'

'How's your mother?' Reg went on. He was in no hurry to leave.

'Not so bad.'

'She never seems to get any letters, does she?'

'No. Well, when you reach that age, most of your friends are dead.'

'How old is she now?'

'She was eighty-six last July.'

'That's a good age. She doesn't go out much, does she?'

'No, not at all. Now, if you'll excuse me, I have to leave to catch my train to work.'

Partridge closed the door and called up the stairs, 'Goodbye, Mother. I'm off to work.'

On his way to the station he stopped at the village shop to get his newspaper.

'Good morning,' said Mr Denton, the shopkeeper. 'How's the old lady?'

'Oh, not too bad, thank you – for her age, that is.'

'Oh, Mr Partridge,' said Mrs Denton, 'there's going to be a meeting in the village hall on Sunday, about–'

21

'I'm sorry, Mrs Denton, I don't like to leave my mother at weekends. I'm at work all week, you see.' He hurried away.

'He lives for his old mother,' said Mr Denton.

'Well,' said his wife, 'she probably won't live much longer. She's been in bed ever since they moved here. And how long ago was that? Three years?'

'Three or four.'

'I don't know what he'll do when she dies.'

'Someone told me that he was talking about going to live in Canada.'

'Well, I expect she'll leave him some money.'

When Mrs Denton expected something, everyone in the village soon heard about it.

◆

In his office that afternoon, Partridge was getting ready to go home when the telephone rang. Mr Brownlow wanted to see him. He hurried to his employer's office.

'Humphrey! Come in and sit down.'

Partridge sat on the edge of a chair. He was going to miss his train.

Mr Brownlow said, 'You know I intended to go to Antwerp next week, for the meeting?'

'Yes.'

'Well, I've just heard that I must go to Rome tomorrow. Parsons is ill and I'm taking his place. So I'd like you to go to Antwerp on Monday.'

'Me? But what about Mr Potter? He has a more responsible position in the company . . .'

'He's too busy. It will be good experience for you. So I'll ask my secretary to change the tickets—'

'No, Mr Brownlow. You see, it's rather difficult.'

'What's the problem?'

'It's my mother. She's very old and I look after her.'

'Oh, it's only for three days, Humphrey. And this is important.'

'I'm sorry, it's not possible. My mother . . .'

There was a pause. Mr Brownlow was looking annoyed.

'All right, then. You can go now, or you'll be late for your train.'

Partridge looked at his watch. 'I think I can just catch it if I hurry.'

'Oh, that's great!' His employer gave a cold smile.

◆

'Mother, I'm home. It's exactly 6.35. I had to run for the train, but I caught it.'

Humphrey Partridge hurried up the stairs, went past his own bedroom and stood by the open door of the second bedroom. There was a smile on his lips as he looked at the empty bed.

◆

It was Monday morning, and Partridge was making his breakfast. He turned on his cooker and prepared to boil an egg. It was an old cooker, but it still worked well.

He looked out of the kitchen window with satisfaction. During the weekend he had dug the garden and planted all the roses.

The door bell rang. It was Reg Carter, the postman, with a big package in his hand.

'Sorry, I couldn't get this through the letterbox.'

Partridge could see that it contained more information about Canada. He would enjoy reading that on the train.

'Oh, and there's this letter too. But nothing for the old lady. Is she all right today?'

'Fine, thank you.' Partridge managed to shut the door behind the postman. He opened the letter.

He looked out of the kitchen window with satisfaction.

When he saw what was in it, he sat down at the bottom of the stairs, feeling weak with shock. He had won a large sum of money in a competition.

◆

'You wanted to see me, Partridge?'

'Yes, Mr Brownlow.'

'Well, be quick, then. I've just flown back from Rome.'

'I've come to tell you I'm leaving.'

'You mean you want to leave the company? This is sudden.'

'Yes, I'm going abroad. To Canada, with my mother.'

'Well, you can go in a month: I need a month's notice.'

'Is it possible for me to go sooner?'

Mr Brownlow suddenly lost his temper. 'Yes! Go today!'

Partridge got home before lunch, feeling pleased. He had telephoned a man who had agreed to sell the house for him; and he had completed the forms necessary for living in Canada. He opened his front door and called out, 'Hello, Mother. I'm home.'

He stopped suddenly as he saw Reg Carter coming out of his kitchen. 'Good God, what are you doing here?'

'I was passing the house, and I saw the smoke.'

'How did you get in?'

'I had to break a window. I've called the police. I explained it all to Sergeant Wallace.'

Partridge's face was white. 'Explained what?'

'About the fire. There was a fire, in your kitchen. You left the cooker on, and the curtains were on fire. I was thinking of your mother upstairs, not able to move. So I put the fire out.'

'Oh thank you, that was very good of you.'

'Then I wanted to see if she was all right. I went upstairs. All the doors were closed. I opened one – your room, I think. Then I opened another. There was a bed there. But there was no one in it.'

'No.'

'There was no one anywhere. The house was empty.'

'Yes.'

The postman stood there, looking at him. 'I thought that was rather strange, Mr Partridge. You told us your mother lived here.'

'She does – I mean she did. She died.'

'Died? When? You said this morning when I asked–'

'She died two days ago.' His face was red now. 'I'm sorry, I can't think straight. It's the shock, you know.'

'I see,' Reg Carter said quietly. 'Well, I must go now.'

◆

It was about a week after the fire. Of course Reg Carter had talked to Mr and Mrs Denton, and they had talked to almost everyone who came into the shop. Sergeant Wallace, the village policeman, had heard a lot of strange stories about Humphrey Partridge. So now he had decided to go and talk to him himself.

Partridge opened the door slowly, and the sergeant went straight into the sitting room. It was full of boxes.

'You're packing your books, I see, Mr Partridge. When are you going to Canada?'

'In about a month.'

'And you're going to buy a house there, I hear?'

'Yes.'

'You're going alone? Your mother's not with you now?'

'No. She . . . she died.'

'Yes. That's what I want to discuss. As you know, this is a small place, and most people take an interest in other people's business. I've been hearing some strange things about you . . . People are saying you killed your mother, to get her money.'

'That's stupid! It's not true!'

'Perhaps. Let me ask you a few questions. First, when did your mother die?'

'Ten days ago. The 11th.'

'Are you sure? The 11th was the day you had the fire.'

'Sorry. Two days before that. It was such a shock . . .'

'Of course. And so the funeral was on the 10th?'

'Some time about then, yes.'

'It's strange that none of the local funeral directors know anything about it.'

'I . . . I used someone from town.'

'I see. And was it a doctor from town who signed the document saying that she was dead?'

'Yes.'

'Do you perhaps have a copy of the document?'

Partridge looked unhappy. 'You know I don't.'

'I'm afraid,' the sergeant said, 'that that suggests there may be something unusual about your mother's death. Now, if a crime has taken place—'

'No crime has taken place!' Partridge cried. 'I haven't got a mother. I never saw my mother. She left me when I was six months old, and I grew up in a children's home.'

'Then who was living upstairs?'

'Nobody. I live alone. I always have lived alone. I hate people. People are always asking you questions. They want to come into your house, take you out for drinks. I can't stand it. I just want to be alone!'

Sergeant Wallace tried to stop him, but now Partridge couldn't stop. 'But people don't allow you to be alone! You have to have a reason. So I invented my mother. I couldn't do things, I couldn't see people, because I had to get back to my mother. I even began to believe in her and talk to her. She never asked questions, she just loved me, and was kind and beautiful. Now you've all killed her!'

Sergeant Wallace took a moment to organize this new information. 'So you're telling me, there never was any mother.

You didn't kill her, because she wasn't here. Hmm. And how do you explain that you suddenly have enough money to go to Canada and buy property?'

'I won a competition. I got the letter on the morning of the fire. That's why I forgot to turn the cooker off. I was so excited.'

'I see.' Sergeant Wallace got up and moved across to the window. 'You've been digging the garden, I notice.'

'Yes, I put those roses in.'

'You plant roses, when you're going away? Hmm!'

◆

A few days later, there was exciting news in the village: Partridge had been put in prison. And the police had dug up his garden, and taken up part of the floor in his house . . . But they hadn't found a body. Then the news came that he had been freed.

It seemed that his strange story to Sergeant Wallace was true. There had been no one else living in the house. He *had* won a large amount of money. And Partridge's mother *was* living in Liverpool, and had been in trouble with the police on several occasions.

Partridge came back to his house and continued preparing for his move to Canada.

Two days before he was going to leave, in the early evening, someone rang his doorbell. It was December, dark and cold. All the villagers were inside their houses.

He did not recognize the woman standing on the doorstep. She was dressed in the clothes of a young woman, but her face was old.

'Hello, Humphrey,' she said.

'Who are you?' He held the door, ready to close it.

The woman laughed. 'No, I don't expect you to recognize me. You were very young when we last met.'

'You're not . . . ?'

'Hello, Humphrey.'

'Yes, I am. Don't you want to give your mother a kiss?'

She pushed her painted face towards him, and Partridge stepped back into the hall. The woman followed him in.

She looked at the packing cases. 'Of course, you're going away. Canada, is it? I read about it in the paper. I read about the money, too.'

'What do you want?' said Partridge.

'I've just come to see my little boy. I was thinking, perhaps you should help your poor old mother now.'

'You never did anything for me. You left me.'

'That was a long time ago. Now I want you to look after me in my old age. Why don't you take your old mother to Canada with you?'

'But you aren't my mother.' He spoke quietly.

'Oh yes, I am, Humphrey.'

'My mother is beautiful and kind. She is nothing like you. You are not my mother!' His hands were on her shoulders, shaking her.

'I'm your mother, Humphrey!' She was laughing at him.

His hands moved to her neck to stop her words. They became tighter and tighter as he shook her.

He opened his hands, and the woman's body fell to the floor. Her mouth opened and her false teeth dropped out.

◆

Next morning Humphrey Partridge went to the police station to see Sergeant Wallace.

'Good morning, Mr Partridge. What can I do for you?'

'Sergeant, about my mother . . . I just wanted to tell you . . . that I did kill her.'

'Oh yes, and then you buried her in the garden?'

'Yes, I did.'

'Fine.'

'I'm telling you I murdered someone,' Partridge said.

'Listen, Mr Partridge,' said the sergeant. 'I'm very sorry about what happened, and you can have a little joke if you like. But now I have other things to do, so . . .'

'You mean I can just go?'

'Do. Please.'

'To Canada?'

'Anywhere you like.'

'All right, then, I'll go.' He left the police station.

Outside, Humphrey Partridge took a deep breath of air, and smiled.

'Right, Mother. We're going to Canada,' he said.

At the Old Swimming Hole   *Sara Paretsky*

I was sitting on a wooden seat at the University of Illinois indoor
swimming pool, and I was not enjoying myself. The air was hot
and wet, the seats were hard and the noise was terrible – shouts
from the swimmers, the officials and the public were making my
head ache.

I had come to watch a swimming competition organized by
Chicago businesses, to collect money for sick people. A number
of companies had sent teams. My old school friend Alicia
Dauphine was in the Berman Airplanes team, and she had asked
me to come and watch her swim. I came, because she was an old
friend – though we didn't often meet now, as we had different
interests.

At school Alicia was interested in only two things: swimming
and engines. She studied engineering at university, and then she
joined Berman Airplanes Company and worked on the design of
planes. And me? I'm a private detective. My business is crime.

Six competitors were standing at the end of the pool, ready to
start the first women's event. From where I sat it wasn't easy to
recognize Alicia. I knew she was wearing a red swimsuit, but
there were three swimmers in red. The pool was divided into
seven lanes. My programme said that Alicia was in lane two.

The woman in the first lane was complaining about
something. The organizer changed the swimmers' positions,
leaving the first lane empty. Now one red suit was in lane two,
one in lane three and one in lane six. I didn't know which one
was Alicia.

The starting gun was fired, and six bodies threw themselves
into the water. There was a perfect start in lane six – that must be
Alicia.

32

The woman in lane two seemed to be having problems. What was wrong? The water around her was turning red. I pushed through the crowd to the side of the pool, kicked off my shoes and jumped in.

I swam under the water to the second lane and pulled the woman to the edge, where someone lifted her out. No, it wasn't Alicia. I shouted to an official to telephone for an ambulance, and knelt down beside the woman. The blood seemed to be coming from her back, below her left shoulder. She was breathing – but then the breathing changed to coughing. By the time the ambulance men arrived to take her to hospital, her breathing had stopped.

◆

It was two hours later, and I was still in my wet clothes. Sergeant McGonnigal had come from the city police to question the witnesses to the murder. He had already talked to the officials, who had the best view of the pool, and now he was talking to me, Victoria (V. I.) Warshawski. He knew me already, of course.

I told him about my part in the events. Before leaving him, I asked what he had learnt about the dead woman. Her name was Louise Carmody, he said; she was twenty-four, and she worked for the Dearborn Bank. Nobody knew of any enemies.

Alicia was waiting for me in the hall. She looked worried. 'Can we talk?' she said.

'After I put on some dry clothes.'

We went back together to my apartment, and I had a hot bath. When I joined her in the living room, she was watching television.

'No news yet,' she said. 'Who was the dead girl?'

'Louise Carmody, from Dearborn Bank. Did you know her?'

'No, I didn't. Do the police know why she was shot?'

I kicked off my shoes and jumped in.

'Not yet. What do you know about it?'

'Nothing. Will they put her name on the news?'

'Probably, if her family has been informed. Why` is this important to you, Alicia?'

'Oh, no special reason.' She looked very anxious.

I didn't believe her. She was hiding something.

'Alicia, do you know who did the shooting? At first you were in lane two. Then they changed the swimmers' positions, and nobody knew who was in which lane. I think they were shooting at *you*, not Louise. Who wants to kill you?'

'No one!' she shouted. She was silent for a minute. Then she said, 'Sorry. It was just such a shock. I'll try to control myself.'

'Good. I'll get some supper.'

I came back with some food, but Alicia didn't want any. She was watching the local news, and her face was white. The swimming-pool murder was the top story, and the name of the dead woman was given.

After that Alicia didn't say much. She asked if she could spend the night with me – she lived an hour's drive out of town. I left her in the sitting room and went to bed. I was still angry that she didn't want to talk to me.

The telephone woke me at 2.30 a.m. A male voice asked for Alicia. 'I don't know who you're talking about,' I said.

'If you don't want to wake her, give her this message. She was lucky yesterday. We want the money by twelve o'clock, or she won't be so lucky a second time.'

I heard the sound of the telephone being put down. Then I heard another similar sound – the telephone in my living room. I got there just as the apartment door was shutting. Alicia had heard the message, and now she was running away. I could hear her feet on the stairs.

◆

I woke up at eight with a bad cold, the result of sitting around in wet clothes. And I was anxious about Alicia. She had clearly borrowed a very large sum of money from someone, if he was ready to kill her. But who?

I telephoned her office; the secretary said she was sick and was staying at home. I tried her home telephone. No answer. Alicia had one brother, Tom, who worked for an insurance company. When I spoke to him he said he hadn't heard from Alicia for weeks. Their father in Florida hadn't heard from her either.

In Chicago there are some big criminal groups. Two years before, I had given some help to Don Pasquale, the leader of one of them. Now he might be able to help *me*. I telephoned Ernesto, who works for him.

'Did you hear about the murder of Louise Carmody at the university swimming pool last night? She was probably shot by mistake. They wanted to kill Alicia Dauphine, who is an old friend of mine. She has borrowed a lot of money from someone. I thought you might know something about it, Ernesto.'

'I don't know her name, Warshawski. I'll ask around, and let you know.'

I couldn't think where Alicia was hiding. Perhaps she was in her own house, but not answering the telephone? I decided to go and have a look.

Her house in Warrenville is near the local school. I left my car outside the school, and walked to the house, past a field where some boys were playing football.

Her car was in the garage, but I couldn't see any sign of life in the house. A cat came out of the trees towards me; it seemed to be hungry. I went round to the back, and there I found that someone had broken in through the kitchen window.

Oh, why hadn't I brought my gun with me? My cold had affected my brain. Feeling nervous, I climbed through the window, and the cat followed me.

In the kitchen and the living room everything was tidy. And in Alicia's study, her computers and electronic equipment were all in place. Clearly, the person who broke in had not come to steal things. Had he come to attack Alicia? I went upstairs, followed by the cat. There was no one in any of the rooms.

As I began to go down the stairs again, I heard a strange sound. Where was it coming from? I realized it was above me. In the ceiling there was a square hole with a wooden cover, leading to the space under the roof. Someone was pushing back the cover. An arm came down, and the arm was holding a gun. I ran down the stairs two at a time.

A heavy noise – someone jumping down to the floor. The sound of the gun being fired, and a pain in my left shoulder. I fell the last few steps to the bottom, but managed to stand up and get to the door. Then I heard the angry cry of the cat, the shout of a man, and a loud crash that sounded like someone falling downstairs. As I opened the door, the cat rushed past me. She had saved my life.

I walked with difficulty to the road, where the boys playing football saw me and came to help. The man with the gun escaped, but they got me to a hospital.

There a young doctor took the bullet out of my shoulder; my thick winter coat had saved me from serious damage. They put me to bed, and I was happy to stay there.

When I woke there was a man in a suit sitting beside the bed.

'Miss Warshawski? I'm Peter Carlton, FBI.'* He showed me his card. 'I know you're not feeling well, but I must talk to you about Alicia Dauphine.'

'Where is she?'

'We don't know. She went home with you after the swimming

*FBI: a goverment department; its duties include solving crimes and the protection of national secrets.

competition yesterday. Is that correct?'

'So the FBI were following her! Why are you interested in her?'

He didn't want to tell me. He only wanted to know exactly what Alicia had said to me.

Finally I said, 'Mr Carlton, you tell me why you're interested in Alicia, and I'll tell you if I know anything connected with that interest.'

He spoke slowly. 'We believe she has been selling Defence Department secrets to the Chinese.'

'No!' I said. 'She wouldn't do that.'

'Some of her designs for plane parts are missing. She's missing. And a Chinese businessman is missing.'

'The designs may be in her home. They could be on a computer disk – she does all her work on computer.'

He told me they had looked through all her computer material at home and at work, and had found nothing.

I told him everything Alicia had said. And I told him about the attack on me – perhaps the man hiding in her house had stolen the disks. He didn't believe me. I was getting tired, and asked him to leave.

Next morning both my cold and my shoulder were much better. The doctors agreed that I could leave hospital.

When I got home I telephoned Ernesto about Alicia. He told me she had borrowed seven hundred and fifty thousand dollars from Art Smollensk. Art Smollensk, the king of gambling. I didn't think Alicia was a gambler, but I didn't know her well these days.

The telephone rang. It was Alicia, talking against a background of noise. 'I saw the news – thank God you're safe, Vic! Don't worry about me. I'm all right.' She put the telephone down before I could ask her anything. Where was she? I thought about the noises in the background. They seemed familiar . . . from a long time ago . . . Suddenly I remembered. It was the sports hall of our old high school. And the swimming teacher, Miss Finley, was a close friend of Alicia's.

◆

The school is in a poor part of South Chicago. There was a guard at the entrance; I showed her my detective's card and said I needed to see the girls' swimming teacher. She let me in, and I found my way to the sports hall, where a lot of girls in orange shirts were doing exercises.

Then I walked through the changing rooms to the swimming pool – when I was at school, we called it 'The Old Swimming Hole'. A few students, boys and girls, were swimming up and down. Alicia was sitting on a chair by the wall, looking at the floor. I joined her.

'Vic!' She looked frightened. 'Are you alone?'

'Yes, I'm alone. What are you doing here?'

'I'm helping Miss Finley with the swimming. She teaches Spanish too, and she's very busy. Is something wrong, Vic?'

'You are in deep trouble. Smollensk is looking for you, and so is the FBI. You can't hide here for ever.'

'The FBI?' She really seemed shocked. 'What do they want?'

'Your designs. They're missing, and the FBI think you sold them to the Chinese.'

'I took the disks home on Saturday evening . . . oh my God! I must get out of here before someone finds me!'

'Where can you go? The FBI and Smollensk are watching all your friends and relations.'

'Tom, too?' She was starting to cry.

'Especially Tom. Alicia, tell me everything. I need to know. I've already been shot once.'

She told me. Tom was the gambler. He had lost everything he owned, but he still couldn't stop. Two weeks ago he had gone to his sister for help. 'I have to help him. You see, our mother died when I was thirteen and he was six. I looked after him, and got him out of trouble. I still do.'

'But how does Smollensk have your name?'

'Is that the man Tom borrowed money from? Tom uses my name sometimes . . .'

'And the designs?'

'Tom came to dinner on Saturday, and he went into the study. I guess he took the disks I had been using, thinking they might be valuable. He knows that my company does a lot of work for the government. It was a gamble – and a gamble that he could sell them before I found out.'

'Alicia, you can't be responsible for Tom for ever. I think we should call the FBI.'

At this point Miss Finley came in. She was surprised to see me. 'Have you come to help Alicia?' she said. I found she knew most of the story. She thought it would be wrong for Alicia to tell the FBI about her own brother.

They went off together. After some time I went to look for them, and found Alicia alone in an office.

'Miss Finley's teaching a Spanish class,' she said. 'Listen. The important thing is to get those disks back. I called Tom, and he agreed to bring them here. I told him I would help him with the money.'

She didn't understand. She didn't see that if the Chinese businessman had left the country, he would have the disks with him. Tom had sold her disks. He no longer had the material.

'Where is he meeting you?'

'At the pool.'

'Now please – you go to Miss Finley's class and I'll meet him at the pool.'

She agreed in the end, but she refused to let me call the FBI. 'I must talk to Tom first. It may all be a mistake.'

I sent the students out of the pool area, and put a notice on the door saying it was closed. I turned out the lights and sat down in a dark corner, my gun in my hand.

At last Tom came in through the boys' changing room. 'Allie! Allie!' he called.

A minute later another man joined him. He looked like one of Smollensk's group. He spoke softly to Tom. Then they went to look in the girls' changing room. When they returned I had moved towards the doors to the main part of the school.

'Tom!' I called. 'It's V. I. Warshawski. I know the whole story. Give me the disks.'

His friend moved his arm. I shot at him and jumped into the water. His bullet hit the place where I had been standing. Another bullet hit the water by my head. I went under the water again. As I came up I heard Alicia's voice.

'Tom, why are you shooting at Vic? Stop it!'

There were some more shots, but not at me. I got to the side of the pool and climbed out. Alicia lay on the floor. Tom stood there silently, while his friend pushed more bullets into his gun.

I ran to him, caught his arm, and stepped as hard as I could on his foot. But Tom — Tom was taking the gun from him. Tom was going to shoot me.

'Drop that gun, Tom Dauphine!' It was Miss Finley, who taught difficult boys in a rough school. Tom dropped the gun.

Alicia lived long enough to talk to the FBI. Tom told his story to the police. He had wanted Smollensk to kill his sister before she said anything about him. Then the world would think *she* had sold her country's secrets.

The FBI arrived five minutes after the shooting stopped. They had been watching Tom, but not closely enough. They were angry that Alicia had been killed while they were on the case. So they said her death was my fault — I hadn't told them where Alicia was. I spent several days in prison. It seemed like a suitable punishment, just not long enough.

Slowly, Slowly in the Wind   *Patricia Highsmith*

Edward (Skip) Skipperton spent most of his life feeling angry. It was his nature. When he was a boy he had a bad temper; now, as a man, he was impatient with people who were slow or stupid. He often met such people in his work, which was to give advice on managing companies. He was good at his job: he could see when people were doing something the wrong way, and he told them in a loud, clear voice how to do it better. The company directors always followed his advice.

Now Skipperton was fifty-two. His wife had left him two years ago, because she couldn't live with his bad temper. She had met a quiet university teacher in Boston, ended her marriage with Skip and married the teacher. Skip wanted very much to keep their daughter, Maggie, who was then fifteen. With the help of clever lawyers he succeeded.

A few months after he separated from his wife, Skip had a heart attack. He was better again in six months, but his doctor gave him some strong advice.

'Stop smoking and drinking now, or you're a dead man, Skip! And I think you should leave the world of business, too – you've got enough money. Why don't you buy a small farm, and live quietly in the country?'

So Skip looked around, and bought a small farm in Maine with a comfortable farmhouse. A little river, the Coldstream, ran along the bottom of the garden, and the house was called Coldstream Heights. He found a local man, Andy Humbert, to live on the farm and work for him.

Maggie was moved from her private school in New York to one in Switzerland; she would come home for the holidays. Skip did stop smoking and drinking: when he decided to do something, he always did it immediately. There was work for him on the farm. He helped Andy to plant corn in the field behind the house; he bought two sheep to keep the grass short, and a pig which soon gave birth to twelve more.

There was only one thing that annoyed him: his neighbour. Peter Frosby owned the land next to his, including the banks of the Coldstream and the right to catch fish in it. Skip wanted to be able to fish a little. He also wanted to feel that the part of the river which he could see from the house belonged to him. But when he offered to buy the fishing rights, he was told that Frosby refused to sell. Skip did not give up easily. The next week he telephoned Frosby, inviting him to his house for a drink. Frosby arrived in a new Cadillac, driven by a young man. He introduced the young man as his son, also called Peter. Frosby was a rather small, thin man with cold grey eyes.

'The Frosbys don't sell their land,' he said. 'We've had the same land for nearly 300 years, and the river's always been ours. I can't understand why you want it.'

'I'd just like to do a little fishing in the summer,' said Skip. 'And I think you'll agree that the price I offer isn't bad – twenty thousand dollars for about 200 metres of fishing rights. You won't get such a good offer again in your lifetime.'

'I'm not interested in *my* lifetime,' Frosby said with a little smile. 'I've got a son here.'

The son was a good-looking boy with dark hair and strong shoulders, taller than his father. He sat there with his arms across his chest, and appeared to share his father's negative attitude. Still, he smiled as they were leaving and said, 'You've made this house look very nice, Mr Skipperton.' Skip was pleased. He had tried hard to choose the most suitable furniture for the sitting room.

'I see you like old-fashioned things,' said Frosby. 'That scarecrow in your field – we haven't seen one of those around here for many years.'

Skip and Andy had made a scarecrow . . .

'I'm trying to grow corn out there,' Skip said. 'I think you need a scarecrow in a cornfield.'

Young Peter was looking at a photograph of Maggie, which stood on the hall table. 'Pretty girl,' he said.

Skip said nothing. The meeting had failed. Skip wasn't used to failing. He looked into Frosby's cold grey eyes and said: 'I've one more idea. I could rent the land by the river for the rest of my life, and then it goes to you – or your son. I'll give you five thousand dollars a year.'

'I don't think so, Mr Skipperton. Thank you for the drink, and – goodbye.'

'Stupid man,' said Skip to Andy, as the Cadillac moved off. But he smiled. Life was a game, after all. You won sometimes, you lost sometimes.

It was early May. The corn which they had planted was beginning to come up through the earth. Skip and Andy had made a scarecrow from sticks joined together – one stick for the body and head, another for the arms and two more for the legs. They had dressed it in an old coat and trousers that Andy had found, and had put an old hat of Skip's on its head.

The weeks passed and the corn grew high. Skip tried to think of ways to annoy Frosby, to force him to rent part of the river to him.

But he forgot about Frosby when Maggie came home for the summer holidays.

Skip met her at the airport in New York, and they drove up to Maine. Skip thought she looked taller; she was certainly more beautiful!

'I've got a surprise for you at home,' Skip said.

'Oh – a horse, perhaps?'

Skip had forgotten she was learning to ride. 'No, not a horse.' The surprise was a red Toyota. He had remembered, at least, that Maggie's school had taught her to drive. She was very excited, and threw her arms round Skip's neck. 'Oh Father your so sweet! And you're looking *very* well!'

Skip and Maggie went for a drive in the new car the next morning. In the afternoon Maggie asked her father if she could go fishing in the stream. He had to tell her that she couldn't, and he explained the reason.

'Well, never mind, there are a lot of other things to do.' Maggie enjoyed going for walks, reading and doing little jobs in the house.

Skip was surprised one evening when Maggie arrived home in her Toyota carrying three fish. He was afraid she had been fishing in the stream, against his instructions.

'Where did you get those?'

'I met the boy who lives there. We were both buying petrol, and he introduced himself – he said he'd seen my photograph in your house. Then we had coffee together–'

'The Frosby boy?'

'Yes. He's very nice. Perhaps it's only the father who's not nice. Well, Pete said, "Come and fish with me this afternoon", so I did. It was fun.'

'I don't – please, Maggie, I don't want you to mix with the Frosbys.'

Maggie was surprised, but said nothing.

The next day, Maggie said she wanted to go to the village to buy some shoes. She was away for nearly three hours. With a great effort, Skip didn't question her.

Then on Saturday morning, Maggie said there was a dance in the nearest town, and she was going.

'I can guess who you're going with,' Skip said angrily.

'I'm going alone, I promise you. Girls don't need a boy to take them to dances now.'

Skip realized that he couldn't order her not to go to a dance. But he knew the Frosby boy would be there. And he knew what was going to happen. His daughter was falling in love with Pete Frosby.

Maggie got home very late that night, after Skip had gone to bed. At breakfast, she looked fresh and happy.

'I expect the Frosby boy was at the dance?' said Skip.

'I don't know what you've got against him, Father.'

'I don't want you to fall in love with an uneducated country boy. I sent you to a good school.'

'Pete had three years at Harvard University.' Maggie stood up. 'I'm almost eighteen, Father. I don't want to be told who I can and can't see.'

Skip shouted at her: 'They're not our kind of people!'

Maggie left the room.

During the next week Skip was in a terrible state. In his business life he had always been able to force people to do what he wanted – but he couldn't think of a way to do that with his daughter.

The following Saturday evening, Maggie said she was going to a party. It was at the house of a boy called Wilmers, who she had met at the dance. By Sunday morning, Maggie hadn't come home. Skip telephoned the Wilmers' house.

A boy's voice said that Maggie had left the party early.

'Was she alone?'

'No, she was with Pete Frosby. She left her car here.'

Skip felt the blood rush to his face. His hand was shaking as he picked up the telephone to call the Frosby house. Old Frosby answered. He said Maggie was not there. And his son was out at the moment.

'What do you mean? Do you mean he was there earlier and he went out?'

'Mr Skipperton, my son has his own ways, his own room, his own key – his own life. I'm not going to–'

Skip put the telephone down.

Maggie was not home by Sunday evening or Monday morning. Skip didn't want to inform the police. On Tuesday there was a letter from Maggie, written from Boston. It said that she and Pete had run away to be married.

. . . You may think this is sudden, but we do love each other, and we know what we're doing. I didn't really want to go back to school. Please don't try to find me – you'll hear from me next week. I was sorry to leave my nice new car.

Love always,

MAGGIE.

For two days Skip didn't go out of the house, and he ate almost nothing. He felt three-quarters dead. Andy was very worried about him. When he needed to go to the village to buy some food, he asked Skip to go with him.

While Andy did the shopping, Skip sat in the car, looking at nothing. But then a figure coming down the street caught his eye. Old Frosby!

He hoped Frosby wouldn't see him in the car, but Frosby did. He didn't pause, but he smiled his unpleasant little smile as he went past. At that moment Skip realized how much he hated Frosby. His blood boiled with anger, and he felt much better: he was himself again. Frosby must be punished! He began to make a plan.

That evening, Skip suggested to Andy that he should go away for the weekend and enjoy himself. 'You've earned a holiday!' he said, and gave him three hundred dollars.

Andy left on Saturday evening, in the car. Skip then telephoned old Frosby, and said it was time they became friends. He asked Frosby to come to Coldsteam Heights again. Frosby was surprised, but he agreed to come on Sunday morning at about eleven for a talk. He arrived in the Cadillac, alone.

Skip acted quickly. He had his heavy gun ready, and as soon as Frosby was inside the door he hit him on the head several times with the end of the gun until Frosby was dead. He then took off his clothes and tied an old cloth round the body. He burned Frosby's clothes in the fireplace, and hid his watch and rings in a drawer.

Then Skip put one arm around Frosby's body, and pulled him out of the house and up the field to the scarecrow. The corn had already been cut. He pulled down the old scarecrow and took the clothes off the sticks. He dressed Frosby in the old coat and trousers, tied a small cloth round his face and pushed the hat onto his head.

When he stood the scarecrow up again it looked almost the same as before. As Skip went back to the house, he turned round many times to admire his work.

He had solved the problem of what to do with the body.

Next he buried Frosby's watch and rings under a big plant in the garden. It was now half past twelve, and he had to do something with the Cadillac. He drove it to some woods a few kilometres away and left it there, after cleaning off all his fingerprints. He hadn't seen anybody.

Soon after he got home a woman telephoned from Frosby's house (his housekeeper, Skip guessed) to ask if Frosby was with him. He told her that Frosby had left his house at about twelve, and he hadn't said where he was going. He said the same thing to the policeman who came to see him in the evening, and to Maggie when she telephoned from Boston. He found it easy to lie about Frosby.

Andy arrived back the next morning, Monday. He had already heard the story in the village, and also knew that the police had found Frosby's car not far away in the woods. He didn't ask any questions.

In the next week Skip spent a lot of time watching the

scarecrow from his upstairs bedroom window. He thought with pleasure of old Frosby's body there, drying – slowly, slowly in the wind.

◆

After ten days the policeman came back, with a detective. They looked over Skip's house and land, and they looked at his two guns. They didn't find anything.

That evening, Maggie came to see him; she and Pete were at the Frosby house. It was hard for Skip to believe she was married. It had all happened so fast.

'Pete's very worried and upset,' she said. 'Was Mr Frosby unhappy when he visited you?'

Skip laughed. 'No, very cheerful! And pleased with the marriage. Are you going to live at the Frosby house?'

'Yes. I'll take some things back with me.'

She seemed cold and sad, which made Skip unhappy.

◆

'I know what's in that scarecrow,' said Andy one day.

'Do you? What are you going to do about it?' Skip asked.

'Nothing. Nothing,' Andy answered with a smile.

'Perhaps you would like some money, Andy? A little present – for keeping quiet?'

'No sir,' Andy said quietly. 'I'm not that kind of man.'

Skip didn't understand. He was used to men who liked money, more and more of it. Andy was different. He was a good man.

The leaves were falling from the trees and winter was coming. The children in the area were getting ready to celebrate the evening of 31st October, when people wore special clothes and had special things to eat, and lit great fires outside and danced around them singing songs.

No one came to Skip's house that evening. There was a party at the Frosbys' house — he could hear the music in the distance. He thought of his daughter dancing, having a good time. Skip was lonely, for the first time in his life. Lonely. He very much wanted a drink, but he decided to keep his promise to himself.

At that moment he saw a spot of light moving outside the window. He looked out. There was a line of figures crossing his field, carrying lights. Anger and fear rushed through him. They were on his land! They had no right! And they were children, he realized. The figures were small.

He ran downstairs and out into the field. 'What do you think you're doing?' he shouted. 'Get off my property!'

The children didn't hear him. They were singing a song. 'We're going to burn the scarecrow . . .'

'Get off my land!' Skip fell and hurt his knee. Now the children had heard him, he was sure, but they weren't stopping. They were going to reach the scarecrow before him. He heard a cry. They had got there.

There were more cries, of terror mixed with pleasure.

Perhaps their hands had touched the body.

Skip made his way back to his house. It was worse than the police. Every child was going to tell his parents what he had found. Skip knew he had reached the end. He had seen a lot of men in business reach the end. He had known men who had jumped out of windows.

Skip went straight to his gun. He put the end in his mouth, and fired. When the children came running back across the field to the road, Skip was dead.

Andy heard the shot from his room over the garage. He had also seen the children crossing the field, and heard Skip shouting. He understood what had happened.

He began walking towards the house. He would have to call the police. Andy decided to say that he didn't know anything

'Get off my property!'

about the body in the scarecrow's clothes. He had been away that weekend, after all.

Woodrow Wilson's Tie   *Patricia Highsmith*

Madame Thibault's Hall of Waxworks attracted a lot of visitors. The front of the building was bright with red and yellow lights, even during the day. Inside the hall were scenes of murders, and other famous historical events, with lifelike figures made out of wax.

Clive Wilkes loved the place, both the outside and the inside. He was a delivery boy for a small supermarket, so he was often able to find some free time during the day to stop and visit the Waxworks. At the entrance to the hall there was a man sitting at a desk selling tickets. Then, after passing through a dark area, you came to the main hall. There in front of you was a bloody murder scene: a girl with long fair hair was pushing a knife into the neck of an old man, who sat at a table eating his dinner. His dinner was a plate of wax meat and wax potatoes.

Next there was the eighteenth-century Frenchman, Marat, who was killed as he sat in his bath; then the murder of President Kennedy, and then a scene in a Nazi prison camp.* Clive loved every scene, and he never got tired of looking at them. But they didn't frighten him as they frightened other people – they made him smile, or even laugh. They were funny. Why not laugh?

One thing which Clive wanted to do very much was to spend a night in the Hall. It wouldn't be too difficult. Clive knew that three people worked there, as well as the ticket seller at the door. There was a rather fat woman with brown hair and glasses, who took the tickets as you went in. There was a man who gave little talks about the different scenes, though not more than half the

---

* Nazi prison camp: a camp run by the German political party which was led by Adolf Hitler and which held power between 1933 and 1945.

people listened to him. And there was another man, small, with black hair, who walked around watching people, to make sure they didn't damage anything.

So one night in November, Clive went in half an hour before the Hall closed, with a cheese sandwich in his pocket. He hid himself in the shadows and listened to the three people as they got ready to leave. The woman, whose name was Mildred, got the moneybox from Fred, the ticket seller, and took it into a room at the back of the hall. Fred left by the front door, the others by the back – first Mildred, then the taller man, then the small one. When Clive heard the door shut and the key turn in the lock, he waited for a moment in the beautiful silence. Then he went to look at the room at the back where they kept their coats, because he had never seen it. They seemed to use it as an office: there was an old desk there. Next to the room was a toilet. In a drawer in the desk was the wooden moneybox, but he wasn't interested in the money.

Clive started to enjoy himself. He found the lights and put them on, so that the scenes were all lit up. Now he was alone, so he could touch things as well as look at them. He stood next to the figures and touched their faces. He ate his sandwich, and sang a few songs.

By two in the morning he was bored, and tried to get out. But both the front door and the back door were locked, and there were no keys anywhere. He used the toilet, and went to sleep on the floor.

He woke up early, and had another look around. He wanted to find something to take home with him. He stopped by a waxwork of President Woodrow Wilson signing a document in 1918, at the end of the First World War. Yes, he would have Woodrow Wilson's tie!

When the hall opened at 9.30, Clive was hiding behind a screen. Members of the public began to come in, but Clive

Yes, he would have Woodrow Wilson's tie!

waited until ten o'clock before he felt it was safe to join them. He left, with Woodrow Wilson's tie in his pocket.

He was half an hour late for work. There was a job waiting for him, so he went off on his bicycle.

Clive lived alone with his mother, who worked in a dress shop. She had no other children, and her husband had left her when Clive was five. He was eighteen now; he had left school early, without completing his education. Then he had spent a year doing nothing much. His mother worried about him and so she was pleased when he got the job at the supermarket.

When Clive came home that evening, he had a story ready for his mother. Last night, he said, he had met a friend and gone back to his house, and his parents had invited him to spend the night there. She accepted this story.

Clive put Woodrow Wilson's tie in the cupboard with his own. It was a beautiful tie, pale grey and expensive. He imagined someone − Mildred, perhaps − looking at the figure of the President and saying, 'Just a minute! What happened to Woodrow Wilson's tie?'

He felt very proud of his adventure, and wanted to tell someone about it, but he had no close friends who he could talk to. By the next day it didn't seem exciting any more.

One afternoon the following week, Clive had another idea. It was a really amusing idea − one that would certainly make the public take notice. When should he do it? Tonight? No, he needed time to plan it.

Two nights later Clive went to the Hall at nine o'clock and bought a ticket. Luckily the ticket seller didn't really look at people; he was too busy.

Clive went straight to Woodrow Wilson, and saw that he was still without a tie. The murder scenes didn't interest him as much as usual. Some real murder scenes would be so much better. He laughed. He would kill the woman first.

As the visitors went out, Clive hid in a dark corner near the office. When Mildred walked past him, in her hat and coat, he stepped forward and put his arm around her neck.

She made only a small 'Ur–rk' sound.

Clive pressed her neck with his hands until her body fell to the floor. Then he pulled her to the dark corner.

'Has Mildred gone?' said one of the men.

'Yes, she's not in the office. Well, I'm going too.'

Clive jumped on him as he passed, and attacked him in the same way. The job was more difficult, because the man fought hard, but Clive managed to knock his head against the wall. It was the taller man, who gave the talks.

'What's happening?' The small, dark man appeared.

This time Clive tried to hit him on the chin. He missed, and hit him in the neck. The man was unconscious now, so Clive was able to knock *his* head against the wall too.

They all seemed to be dead. Blood was pouring from the heads of the two men, and the woman was bleeding a little from the mouth. Clive found the keys in the second man's pocket. There was a pocketknife there, which he took too.

Then the taller man moved a little. Clive opened the pocketknife and pushed it into his neck four times. They were all dead now, and that was certainly real blood coming out, not the red paint of the wax figures.

Clive turned on the lights which lit up the scenes, and began the interesting job of choosing the right places to put the bodies.

The woman should certainly go in Marat's bath. Clive thought of taking off her clothes, but decided against it, because she would look much funnier sitting in a bath with a coat and hat on. He took the figure of Marat out of the bath, carried it into the office and placed it on the desk.

Then he carried Mildred to the bath and put her in. God, she looked funny!

Now for the men. He decided that the man whose neck was cut would look good in the place of the old man who was having dinner. After all, the girl with the long fair hair was pushing a knife into his neck. The figure of the old man was in a sitting position, so Clive put him on the toilet. He looked so funny there, with a knife in one hand and a fork in the other, waiting for something to eat. Clive laughed and laughed.

Last, the little man. Clive looked around and noticed the Woodrow Wilson scene. The figure of the President was sitting at a large desk, signing a paper; that was an excellent place, Clive thought, for a man whose head was cut open and bleeding. He managed to take the wax pen out of Wilson's fingers, carry him into the office and put him on the chair at the desk. His arms were in a position for writing, so Clive found a pen on the desk to put into his right hand.

Now he could put the little man in Woodrow Wilson's place. He lifted him up onto the chair, but his head fell forward onto the desk, and Clive could not make his hand hold the pen.

At last it was done. Clive smiled. Then he realized that every part of his body was tired. Now that he had the keys he could get out, go home, and sleep well in his own bed. He wanted to be ready to enjoy tomorrow.

There was some blood on his coat, so he must throw it away somewhere. But he needed a coat. He took one off a wax figure which was about his size, and put that on. Then he used the inside of his own coat to clean off any possible fingerprints from places he had touched. He turned off the lights, and found his way to the back door. He locked it behind him, and dropped the keys on the ground. In the street was a box with some old newspapers, empty cans and plastic bags in it, where he hid the coat.

Clive slept very well that night. The next morning, he was standing across the street from the Hall when the ticket seller

59

arrived just before 9.30. By 9.35 only three people had gone in, but Clive could not wait any longer, so he crossed the street and bought a ticket.

The ticket seller was telling people, 'Just go in. Everybody is late this morning.' He went inside to put on the lights, and Clive followed him.

There were four other customers now. They looked at Mildred in her hat and coat sitting in Marat's bath without noticing anything strange about her. Two more people came in.

At last, by the Woodrow Wilson scene, a woman said to the man with her: 'Was someone shot when they signed that document at the end of the war?' There was blood, real blood, on the papers on the desk. By now they were dark red.

'I don't know. I don't think so,' the man answered.

Clive wanted very much to laugh, but he managed not to.

Suddenly a woman cried out in terror, and at the same time a man shouted, 'My God, it's *real*!'

Another man was examining the body with its face in the meat and potatoes. 'The blood's *real*! It's a dead man!'

The ticket seller, Fred, came in. 'What's the trouble?'

'There are two dead bodies here! *Real* ones!'

Now Fred looked at Marat's bath. 'Good God! Good *God*! *Mildred*!'

'And this one! And this one here!'

'I must call the police!' said Fred. 'Could you all, please – just leave?'

He ran into the office, where the telephone was, and Clive heard him cry out. He had seen Woodrow Wilson at the desk, of course, and Marat.

Clive thought it was time to leave, so he did. No one looked at him as he made his way out.

That was all right, he thought. That was good.

He decided to go to work and to ask for the day off. He told

'The blood's real!'

his employer he felt ill, and put his hand on his stomach. Old Mr Simmons had to let him go.

Clive wanted to take a long bus ride somewhere. He didn't know why he wanted to do this, but the need was very strong. He had brought all his cash with him, about twenty-three dollars, and now he bought a ticket for a bus going west − for seven dollars, one way. This took him, by the evening, to a town in Indiana.

There was a café here where the bus stopped. As he went in, he saw newspapers on sale. There it was, in big letters:

MYSTERY KILLER: THREE DEAD IN WAXWORKS HALL

He bought a paper and read it at the bar, drinking beer.

This morning at 9.30 ticket man Fred Keating and several visitors to Madame Thibault's Waxworks discovered three real dead bodies. They were the bodies of Mrs Mildred Veery, aged 41, George Hartley, 43, and Richard MacFadden, 37, all employed at the Hall. Police believe the murders happened at about ten yesterday evening. Because the bodies were put in place of wax figures, police are looking for a killer with a sick mind.

Clive laughed over that. 'Sick mind!' But he was sorry that there were no details about the really amusing things: the old man sitting on the toilet, the man signing the document with his head broken and bleeding.

Two men were standing at the bar beside him.

'Did you read about the murders at the Waxworks?' he asked one of them.

'Not really.' He didn't seem interested.

'You see, I did them,' said Clive. He pointed to a picture of the bodies. 'That's my work.'

'Listen, boy,' said the man. 'We're not troubling you, and don't you trouble us.' They moved away from Clive.

Clive slept in the street that night. On the road the next day he waved at a passing car, which took him to another town, nearer his hometown. That day's newspapers did not have any more news about the murders. In another café that evening he had a similar conversation, this time with two young men. They didn't believe him, either.

Next day he stopped a few more cars, and finally reached his hometown. He went straight to the police station.

'I have something important to say about a murder,' he told the policeman sitting at a desk. He was sent to the office of a police officer who had grey hair and a fat face. Clive told his story.

'Where do you go to school, Clive?'

'I don't. I'm eighteen.' He told him about his job.

'Clive, you've got troubles, but they're not the ones you're talking about,' said the officer.

Clive had to wait in a small room in the police station, and nearly an hour later a doctor was brought in. Then his mother. They didn't believe him. They said he was just telling this story to attract attention to himself.

'Clive needs a man around the house,' his mother told them; 'someone who can teach him to behave like a man. Since he was fourteen he's been asking me questions like "Who am I?" and "Am I a person?"'

The policeman told Clive he must see the doctor twice a week for treatment.

Clive was very angry. He refused to go back to the supermarket, but found another delivery job.

'They haven't found the murderer, have they?' Clive said to the doctor on one of his visits. 'You're all stupid – stupid!'

The doctor only laughed at him.

There was one thing which might help to prove his story: Woodrow Wilson's tie, which was still in his cupboard. But he wasn't going to show it to these stupid people. As he delivered things on his bicycle, as he had supper with his mother, he was planning.

Next time, he would do something really big. He would take a gun up to the top of a high building, and shoot at the people in the street. Kill a hundred people at least. Then they would take notice of him – then they would realize that he was a *person!*

The Absence of Emily   *Jack Ritchie*

When I married my second wife, Emily, I went to live in her house in northern California. It's a big house with a lot of land around it, just outside a small town. The next house is almost exactly the same, and that belongs to Emily's sister Millicent.

Millicent and Emily. Sisters. But completely different in looks and in character. Millicent is tall and rather thin. She is very strong-minded and likes to control everyone around her, including Emily. She wasn't at all pleased when I came and took Emily away from her influence.

Emily is rather short, and – well, fat. As she says, she weighs eleven or twelve kilos too much. She doesn't claim to be very clever, and usually she does what other people want. Not always, though.

For three weeks now, Emily had been away. But Millicent had been watching me closely. She was with me now, drinking coffee in our sitting room.

The telephone rang, and I answered it. 'Yes?'

'Hello, dear, this is Emily.'

'Emily – er – what is your surname?'

'Oh, really, dear. Emily, your wife.'

'I'm sorry, you must have a wrong number.' I put the telephone down.

Millicent was watching me. 'You look as white as a sheet. You seem frightened. Shocked. Who telephoned?'

'It was a wrong number.'

Millicent drank some coffee. 'Oh, Albert, I thought I saw Emily in town yesterday. But that's not possible.'

'Of course it's not. Emily is in San Francisco.'

'Yes, but where in San Francisco?'

'She didn't say. She's visiting friends.'

'Emily doesn't have any friends in San Francisco! I know all her friends. When will she be back?'

'She wasn't sure when it would be.'

'I've heard, Albert, that your first wife died in a boating accident? She fell out of the boat and died in the water?'

'I'm afraid so. She couldn't swim.'

'And you were the only witness to the accident.'

'I believe so. No one else ever came forward.'

'Did she leave you any money, Albert?'

'That's nothing to do with you, Millicent.'

In fact Cynthia had fifty thousand dollars of life insurance and one sailing boat. Poor Cynthia. She had taken her boat out alone that day. I had seen the accident from the boat club, and rushed out in another boat, but it was too late to save her.

Millicent finished her coffee and left.

When she had gone, I went for a walk through the woods behind the house. I walked to an open space between the trees, which had a little stream running through it. How peaceful it was here. Quiet. A place to rest. I had been coming here often in the last few days.

I sat down on a fallen tree near the stream and thought about Emily and Millicent. Their houses and land were very similar, so you would expect them to be equally rich. But this was not the situation, as I discovered after my marriage. Emily owned her house and the land around it, but she could not afford to employ people to look after them.

Millicent, on the other hand, employed a lot of people in her house, and even a lawyer to look after her money. She must have a million dollars, at least.

On Tuesday afternoons I usually go to the supermarket in town. Today, in the car park, I saw a small, rather fat woman across the street walking away from me. She wore a purple dress and a

I saw a small, rather fat woman across the street walking away from me.

brown hat. It was the fourth time I'd seen her in the last ten days. I hurried across the street. She turned the corner and I started to run. When I reached the corner she was nowhere in sight.

I was standing there when a car stopped beside me.

It was Millicent. 'What are you doing, Albert? I saw you running – I've never seen you run before.'

'Oh, I was just taking a little exercise.' I was still breathing hard as I walked back to the supermarket.

The next morning, when I returned from my walk to the stream, I found Millicent in the sitting room, pouring some coffee for herself.

'I've been in the bedroom looking at Emily's clothes,' Millicent said. 'I didn't see anything missing.'

'Why should anything be missing? Has there been a thief in the house?'

'Don't tell me that Emily went off to stay with friends in San Francisco without any luggage!'

'She had luggage. Though not very much.'

'What was she wearing when she left?'

'I don't remember,' I said.

That evening, as I prepared for bed, I looked inside Emily's cupboard. What could be done with her clothes? Perhaps I should give some away?

I woke up at two in the morning – bright moonlight was shining on my face. I dressed, and went out to the hut in the garden. I needed something for digging a hole.

I chose a spade with a long handle, put it on my shoulder and began walking towards the stream.

I was nearly there when I stopped. I shook my head slowly and returned to the hut. I put the spade away and went to bed.

The next morning Millicent came to see me while I was having breakfast. She brought in the morning post, which had just come. It included one small blue envelope addressed to me.

The writing seemed familiar. The postmark was our local town.

I opened the envelope and pulled out a sheet of paper.

Dear Albert,

I miss you so very much. I shall return home soon, Albert. Soon.

EMILY.

I put the letter and the envelope into my pocket.

'Well?' Millicent asked. 'I thought I recognized Emily's writing on the envelope. Did she say when she'll be back?'

'That is not Emily's writing. It's a letter from my aunt in Chicago.'

'I didn't know you had an aunt in Chicago.'

'Don't worry, Millicent, I do have an aunt in Chicago.'

That night I was in bed, but awake, when the telephone beside my bed rang.

'Hello, my sweet. This is Emily.'

'You are not Emily. You are someone else.'

'Don't be silly, Albert! Of course this is me, Emily.'

'You can't be Emily. I know where she is, and she couldn't telephone at this time of night.'

'You think you know where I am? No, I'm not there now. It was too uncomfortable. So I left, Albert.'

I got out of bed and dressed. I went downstairs to the study and made myself a drink. I drank it slowly.

It was nearly one o'clock in the morning when I went to the garden hut again, and took out the spade.

This time I went all the way to the space between the trees. I stopped beside the highest tree of all.

I began taking big steps, counting at the same time. 'One, two, three, four . . .' I stopped at sixteen.

Then I began digging.

I had been digging for nearly five minutes when I heard a

shout, and suddenly there were people all around me, shining lights in my face. I recognised some of the people who worked for Millicent, including her lawyer.

Now Millicent herself stepped forward. 'So you wanted to be sure she was really dead, Albert! And the only way to do that was to return to the place where you buried her.'

'I am looking for old Indian knives,' I said. 'There's a belief that if you find one in the light of the moon, it will bring you good luck.'

Millicent took no notice of this. She pointed to some people I didn't know. 'These are private detectives,' she said. 'They have been watching you twenty-four hours a day, ever since I guessed what really happened to Emily.' She pointed at a small, rather fat woman. 'That's Mrs Macmillan. She was the woman in the purple dress, and she copied Emily's writing. And this is Miss Peters. She is good at copying voices, and she was the voice of Emily you heard on the telephone.'

There were also two detectives, who had brought their own spades. Now they began digging in the hole which I had started.

'We knew you were getting worried, Albert,' said Millicent. 'You almost dug her up last night, didn't you? But then you changed your mind. That was lucky, because last night I didn't have so many people to watch you. Tonight we were ready and waiting.'

The detectives dug for about fifteen minutes and then paused for a rest.

'This ground is very hard!' said one.

They went on digging until the hole was two metres deep.

'Nothing has been buried here!' said the other. 'The only thing we found was an old Indian knife.'

I smiled at Millicent. 'What makes you think I *buried* Emily?'

I left them and returned to the house.

'What makes you think I buried Emily?'

I had guessed from the beginning that Millicent was responsible for the false 'Emily' that had appeared to me in different forms. It was all part of her plan. What had been her aim? Well, she believed that I had killed her sister. So she wanted to frighten me until I broke down and said, 'Yes, yes, I killed her!'

I had been playing a game too: I wanted her to think I was frightened. And, of course, I wanted her to think I had buried the body in that place in the woods.

Now I was in a strong position. She had called me a murderer in front of all those witnesses – I could take the matter to a court of law, and demand a large sum of money from her. But she wouldn't want to let that happen: she wouldn't want the world to know she had been stupid. She would prefer to pay those people to keep silent. Would that be possible? Well, it would help if I supported her story, and said that nothing had happened at all.

And I would do that for Millicent. If she gave me some money – a large amount of money.

At the end of the week, my telephone rang.

'This is Emily. I'm coming home now, dear.'

'Oh, great.'

'Did anyone miss me?'

'They certainly did!'

'You haven't told anyone where I've been these last four weeks, have you, Albert? Especially not Millicent?'

'I told her you were visiting friends in San Francisco.'

'Oh dear, I don't know anybody in San Francisco. Did she believe you?'

'I don't think so.'

'Well, I couldn't tell her I was going to a health farm, to lose weight! I would be ashamed! And I wasn't sure that I would manage it. But I have, Albert, I have! I've lost fourteen kilos! My figure must be as good as Cynthia's now!'

'Well done, Emily! That's great!'

Why is Emily jealous of my first wife? They each have their place in my heart.

'Yes . . . but now none of my clothes will fit me. I'll have to get a lot of new clothes. Do you think we can afford it, Albert?'

Ah, we can now. With some help from Millicent.

The Inside Story   *Colin Dexter*

It was 8.50 on the morning of Monday, 15th February, 1993.

'Hurry, Lewis!' said Inspector Morse. Sergeant Lewis was driving him through the streets of Oxford and Morse was looking at a street plan. They were on their way to the scene of a murder.

'That's it, Lewis: Jowett Place. What number is it?'

'Fourteen. Where those two police cars are, sir.'

The Oxford City Police had received a telephone call an hour or two earlier from a man called Paul Bayley, living at 14 Jowett Place, who had discovered a murder. That morning, he told them, he had found that he had no milk for breakfast, so he had gone down to borrow some milk from the woman who lived in the flat below him, Sheila Poster. He had knocked on the door — found the door unlocked — walked in, and there ...

Now it was Morse who looked down at the woman lying on her back, just inside the living room. She was lying in a very large pool of blood. It appeared that she had been killed by a knife through the heart.

Big brown eyes looked out at them from a pale face; her hair was long and dark.

'Beautiful girl,' said Lewis quietly.

Morse turned his eyes away. He always turned away from the sight of violent death.

The police doctor had arrived, and was ready to examine the body. 'You can look at her now,' Morse said to her.

The house had been divided into two flats; Sheila Poster had rented the ground floor, and the floor above was rented by Paul Bayley. Morse and Lewis went upstairs now to talk to him.

Bayley was sitting beside a policeman in his untidy living room. He was a young man of twenty-seven or twenty-eight; he was tall, with long, dirty hair, but he was quite good-looking. Morse disliked him immediately. He had studied History at one of the Oxford University colleges, he told them, but he didn't have a job just now. As he spoke, his fingers were moving all the time – short, fat, rather dirty fingers they were.

On the evening before, he said, he had been out drinking with friends. He had not left the King's Arms in Broad Street until it closed at ten o'clock, and then he had gone back with a friend to her flat. In fact he'd slept there, before returning to Jowett Place at about 7.15 that morning. He had already told the police the rest of the story.

'You slept with a woman last night?'

'Yes.' He looked at the floor.

'We shall have to know her name – the sergeant here will have to check with her. Now, what can you tell us about Sheila Poster?'

'She was at St Hilda's College at one time – studied English Literature. I don't think she had a job.'

'Did you know her well?'

'Er . . . no, not really.'

Morse and Lewis went back to Sheila Poster's flat. The police doctor was still in the murder room, examining the body, so they had a look at the other rooms – a kitchen and a bedroom, both very small.

There was not much to see in the bedroom. The big cupboard contained her clothes and some cheap shoes. On the table beside the bed were a lamp, a clock, a box full of cheap jewellery and a book.

The title of the book was *Thoughts on Writing Stories*. When Morse picked it up, it opened at a page where a leather bookmarker had been placed. Some sentences had been marked with a yellow pen:

Of course the writer will make use of real people and events from his own experience. But to these he will add imaginary ones, which will give his story its special power.

Lewis picked up the bookmarker, which had 'Greetings from Erzincan' on it.

'Where's Erzincan?'

'Eastern Turkey, I think. Wasn't there an earthquake near there last year?'

From the room above they could hear the sound of someone walking up and down, up and down. Morse looked up at the ceiling. It must be Bayley.

The doctor had finished her examination of the body, and Morse wanted to hear her opinion.

'It was a sharp knife, I think. A lot of blood, as you can see. The time of death was probably eight to ten hours ago. Eleven o'clock, twelve o'clock last night? I'll be able to give you a more exact time later.'

◆

It was almost twelve o'clock when Morse gave the order for the body to be taken away. The police had finished their work on the flat. Lewis, with two policemen, had been sent out to check Bayley's story, to question the neighbours, and to discover something about Sheila Poster's past. And Morse himself now stood alone, looking round the room in which she had been murdered.

He could see that there was not much to find there. All the drawers of the desk were empty; probably the murderer had taken everything away. No handbag, no documents, nothing.

Or was there something?

Above the desk was a wooden board with some picture postcards fixed to it. There was also a card which announced a crime-story competition, organised by the Oxford Library. It had an address on it, which Morse wrote down. Then he took down all the postcards, and looked at the backs. Only one, a picture of Cairo, had a message on it:

'Cairo is hot and unpleasant, but I miss you – R.'

It looked like a man's writing.

On the floor beside the desk there were some piles of magazines, which didn't look very interesting.

There were also some bookshelves, with books of poems on them. Morse noticed one of his favourites. He took it out, and another postcard fell out of it. It had a photograph of San Jose, in California, on the front, and on the back were written two lines of a poem:

And far away are you, my love,
And the sea's between us two.

The writing was the same as that on the Cairo card.

Lewis came back into the room a little later, and began reading from his notebook:

'Sheila Emily Poster, age twenty-five; comes from Bristol; both parents dead, no brothers or sisters; second-class degree in English from St Hilda's, 1990; worked for a time with the University Earth Sciences Department; has been in this flat for ten months.'

'Good!' said Morse. 'Now I'd like you to look through these.' He pointed to the piles of magazines, and went out to get some lunch.

Lewis was still working when Morse came back.

'Have you found anything?'

It looked like a man's writing.

'Just one thing.' He picked up an old copy of *Oxford Week* and pointed to an advertisement which had been marked with a cross in pencil.

Cleaner wanted for ten hours a week. Educated person preferred. Box 733.

'I telephoned the paper about the box number, sir,' said Lewis, 'but the girl told me they didn't keep records for more than three months.'

'A pity. Well, I'll leave you to finish the magazines.'

Morse had remembered the crime story competition. He decided to go himself to the address given on the card. He took a taxi there, and found it was the home of the head of the Oxford Book Association.

'We haven't received many stories yet, because there's still another month to the closing date,' he told Morse. 'These are the names of the writers.' He showed him a list of nine names. Sheila Poster was not one of them.

'Of course, some don't use their real names. Would you like to see their addresses?' He gave Morse another list.

Yes, there it was – (7) ELISSA THORPE, 14 Jowett Place.

'Can you let me have number seven, please?'

ELISSA THORPE . . . SHEILA POSTER – he realized that the two names were made up of the same letters!

When he returned to his office, there was a message for him from the police doctor: she had found that Sheila Poster had been expecting a baby in about six months.

But Morse had something else to think about.

He sat down in his armchair and began to read Sheila's story. And as he read, he remembered the words from the book beside her bed: 'The writer will use real people and events . . . he will add imaginary ones . . .'

The story was clearly typed:

DEATH IN NORTH OXFORD by Elissa Thorpe

I saw the advertisement in the local newspaper:

Cleaner needed three mornings a week, must be careful worker. Write to Mrs Gilbey, 5 Squitchey Lane, N. Oxford.

Well, why not? I thought. I certainly needed some money, now that I'd lost my job. And there was the baby I was expecting.

But that wasn't the real reason, of course. The real reason was that I wanted to meet Mrs Gilbey, wife of Mr John Gilbey . . . Can you guess why? You can't? Not yet?

You will.

I wrote to Mrs Gilbey (signing the letter Vera Carr instead of my real name, Marie Lawson) and she telephoned, asking me to come and see her. Her voice was cold. I guessed that she would be a real North Oxford lady.

And she was.

I took a bus out to Squitchey Lane, and found Number 5. It was a fine old house, built mostly of wood, with a well-kept garden.

Mrs Gilbey didn't smile when she opened the front door. She took me into the kitchen and gave me a cup of coffee, while she asked me a lot of questions. I realized that she was a woman with a high opinion of herself and a low opinion of most other people. But she offered me the job.

'Do you want me to clean the whole house?' I asked.

'No, you needn't clean my husband's study. He's abroad.'

'Oh, is he?' I said politely. I didn't want to seem too interested in her husband.

'Yes, he's giving a series of talks in America.'

She took me to the front door, and I said goodbye. I looked back at her standing there: tall, well-dressed and even quite young - younger than I had expected.

And yes, I have to say it - very attractive.

I spent nine hours a week at the house. This was only just enough time to finish all the work I had to do. The most difficult room to clean was Mrs Gilbey's study. It was at the back of the house, built out into the garden, with big windows and a glass door. At the bottom of that was a small door for the cat, about twenty centimetres square. Every surface in the room, even the floor, was covered with untidy piles of books and papers.

The sitting room had a lot of books in it too, but they were on shelves. On the Wednesday morning of my third week I was cleaning this room when my employer came to tell me that she had to go out for two hours. I had an idea.

I took a book from the shelf beside me and blew along the top, making a cloud of dust. 'Would you like me to dust the books?'

For a moment I thought I saw hate in her cold grey eyes.

'Yes, if you put them back exactly as you found them.'

'I'll try, madam.'

'Don't try. Do it!'

It was going to be a big job: bookshelves covered three sides of the room. In the middle of the morning I went to the kitchen to make some coffee. Outside the window I saw the young man who sometimes came to work in the garden.

I held my coffee cup up to the window, inviting him to join me. He came in. He was really quite good-looking – except for his hands, with their short, fat fingers.

I asked him how well he knew Mrs Gilbey.

'Oh, quite well.' He smiled, like a man with a secret. Then he bent forward and kissed me on the lips.

I was working on the books on the third wall when Mrs Gilbey came back. As I heard the front door open, I took a piece of paper from my pocket and pushed it between two books. I had written a few words on it, with a green pen:

Dearest J

Please try to keep this page somewhere, to help you to remember our love.

MARIE.

I pulled out a book just as Mrs Gilbey entered the room. The paper fell to the floor, and she picked it up.

Holding the paper, she left the room without a word.

At home I wrote another letter with that green pen, to my lover – to tell him that he was going to be the father of my child. I asked him to remember his promise to end his marriage and marry me. Now do you understand who he was?

I addressed the letter to Squitchey Lane. I wanted his wife to read it – she would open it, I knew, before sending it to him. She would recognize the green writing.

The next day I had to go to the hospital to be examined, to make sure my baby was all right. I had to wait a long time, and I began thinking. I thought of a good way to end John Gilbey's marriage – I could kill Mrs Gilbey! It would be easy – I had a plan!

The following Thursday I received two letters.

The first was from the hospital. I was fine. The baby was fine. I felt almost happy.

The postmark on the second letter was Los Angeles. It was from the father of my child. 'Don't be stupid!' he wrote. 'You must not have that baby. I will pay for the operation, but then there must be a complete break between us. I will see you after my return, which is on the afternoon of Saturday 13th.'

The following day, Friday, was going to be my last day as a cleaner, and that morning I completed my preparations. At first I had intended to kill only Mrs Gilbey; but now I had decided to include Him as well. If they were together.

On Saturday I received another letter, from Mrs Gilbey.

Dear Marie Lawson,

Oh yes, I do know your real name! You see, my husband told me all about you, and showed me a photograph of you. You really must be very stupid - you thought you were watching *me*, and all the time I was watching *you*! I wanted to know why you had come here.

I am writing now to tell you not to return here. Also to thank you for your letter to my husband. (I made a copy of it before sending it to him.) You see, I intend to end my marriage, and marry someone else. My lawyer informs me that your letter will be very useful when the case goes to court.

V. GILBEY (MRS).

Stupid. Both of them had called me stupid.

That Saturday night, very late, I entered the front garden of 5 Squitchey Lane, and waited until the light was turned out in Mrs Gilbey's bedroom. I knew they must both be in there, because I had seen two figures behind the curtains. After another hour I made my way silently into the back garden, and to the door of the study.

Behind the cat-door I had placed a big pile of papers. Now I lit a match, and pushed it through the hole until it touched the papers. They began to burn immediately. There were more papers beside them, and soon those were burning too. I ran away from the house and out of the garden.

From fifty metres away I could see that the sky behind the house was pink. But I didn't stay to watch.

The story of the fire was in Monday's *Oxford News*. It said that the house had been completely destroyed. Two bodies had been found, but they were unrecognizable. The police thought they were the bodies of Mr John Gilbey, who had just returned from America, and his wife Valerie.

There was more about the fire in Tuesday's paper.

Late on Monday evening the Oxford police were very surprised to receive a telephone call from Mr John Gilbey, who was at Heathrow Airport. He had not left America on Saturday after all, and had telephoned his wife to inform her of this. He had just arrived in England, and he had read about the fire in a newspaper.

So, whose was the second body in the Gilbeys' house? It was a complete mystery.

But it wasn't a mystery to me. I could guess who was in Mrs Gilbey's bedroom that night.

Mr Gilbey had telephoned his wife on Saturday – so she had known he would not be in England. It was her last chance to spend a night with her good-looking young lover.

And Mr Gilbey had also telephoned me.

Now I shall wait a little, until the worst of the shock has passed. And then I shall telephone him, and suggest a meeting. Perhaps we could have a life together after all. What do you think?

Lewis came into Morse's office just before four o'clock.

'There's not much to report, sir. I found a postcard on the board in her room – it's probably from a boyfriend.'

'I saw it.'

'And another card – I think the writing is the same.'

It was a picture of Tashkent, in Uzbekistan; the message on the back was 'Travelling 250 K East'.

'I found it in her book of maps,' Lewis said. 'I was looking for Erzincan.'

Morse now picked up Sheila Poster's story, and explained where he had got it. 'I don't think it's a very good story, but it should give us some clues. I want you to read it. You can go and have a sandwich at the same time.'

Lewis returned an hour later. 'Well, there are a lot of clues, sir, but I expect the names are all false.'

'Probably, but you can check. And telephone some university departments and ask for the names of men who have given talks recently in America.'

Lewis went off. Morse returned to the murder room at 14 Jowett Place, where a policeman was guarding the door: he felt there was something there that he had missed. But he could find nothing more in that sad room. He sat down in the only comfortable chair and went to sleep.

Next morning, Lewis reported that he had failed to discover anything.

'I failed, too,' said Morse.

'So what do we do next?'

'Perhaps we should try and think about the *reason* for the crime. And about what Sheila Poster was trying to tell us – trying to tell *herself* – in the story she wrote.' He paused for a minute, and then began speaking slowly. 'Let's think of her situation. She had a job, and then she lost it. Now she hasn't any money – everything she owns is cheap. She meets a man, and falls in love with him. He's married – but he tells her he'll take her away somewhere, and she believes him. Then by chance she finds an advertisement his wife has put in the local paper. She goes to work there – she's jealous of her. Then the husband changes his mind, and leaves her. Now she hates both of them, and wants to destroy them. But she finds she doesn't really want to destroy the father of her child. So in her story she changes things and gives the wife a lover of her own, and destroys both of *them*. Now the husband is alone, and she hopes to win him back.

'But the real–life husband wants to break with Sheila. He wants to keep the whole thing secret – perhaps it's important for his job. He goes to see her, but she won't do what he wants. She says she'll tell everyone about the baby. He loses his temper – and then he knifes her ...'

'*Who* knifes her?' asked Lewis quietly.

'Yes, who? I just don't know.' Morse looked angry, but there was something that Lewis wanted to ask him.

'I hope you don't mind, sir, but could I go home for an hour or two at lunchtime? You see, our kitchen wall is in a terrible state – it looks like the after effects of an earthquake – and we've asked someone to come and–'

He stopped. Morse was looking at him very strangely.

'Lewis, my old friend, you've found the answer! Now I see it ... I see all of it ... Yes, of course you can go home!'

◆

Lewis returned three hours later, with the news that his house was not going to fall down after all.

Morse was looking very cheerful, too. On the desk in front of him were some postcards and the bookmarker from Sheila's flat.

He picked up the bookmarker. 'Clue number one, from Erzincan, Turkey. Numbers two, three and four' – he pointed to them – 'cards from Uzbekistan, Cairo and California. All places where there have been *earthquakes* recently. Clue number five, the fact that Sheila had worked in the Earth Sciences Department here. I was blind not to think about that before. And then you, Lewis, start talking about an earthquake in your kitchen–'

'Actually, sir, it was the ground under the house–'

'So I telephoned the secretary of the Earth Sciences Department, and asked which of their people had been giving talks in America recently. She said nobody had. Then she thought for a moment and said someone had just got back from a six-week visit to Sacramento, in California, where a group of scientists from all over the world had been discussing . . . what do you think?'

'Earthquakes!' cried Lewis. 'What's his name, sir? Does his first name begin with R?'

'It does. Dr Robert Grainger, lives at Cumnor Hill.'

◆

'Why do you think he did it?' asked Lewis, as they drove towards Cumnor Hill, a few kilometres out of Oxford.

'Do you mean Grainger? Well, he had one possible reason. He was hoping to be made Head of Department – the biggest prize of all. But–'

'Sheila Poster was going to ruin everything,' said Lewis.

Morse started to speak, but changed his mind.

When they reached Dr Grainger's house, they crossed the well-kept garden and knocked on the front door. It was opened by a man of about forty-five, thin, with grey hair.

'Dr Grainger?' Morse showed him his police card.

'Yes. You had better come in.' He led them into a sitting room. They sat down, and Morse began asking him questions.

Grainger spoke slowly, and without feeling. Yes, he knew that Sheila Poster had been murdered. He'd read it in the *Oxford News*. Yes, they had been lovers; she had wanted him to leave his wife and go to live with her. She had told him about the baby, but he didn't believe her. His wife knew all about it. In fact, Sheila had managed to get a job as a cleaner in the house while he was away, and had tried to poison the relationship between his wife and himself. She had been working there until about two weeks ago. Now his wife was very upset about the murder.

'Dr Grainger?'

'Where were you on Sunday night?' asked Morse quietly.

'I was in America – that's where I was.'

'And you can prove that?'

Grainger went over to a desk near Lewis's chair, where a large envelope lay beside a wedding photograph. 'Here are my travel documents.' He gave the envelope to Morse. 'As you can see, I arrived back only yesterday afternoon – Monday. The plane landed at 4.15. I caught the bus to Oxford, and got here at about 6.45.'

'That should be easy to check. Now, sir, could I speak to Mrs Grainger?'

'No, I'm sorry, she's gone out. I don't know where.'

'I see. It would help us, sir, if you knew where Mrs Grainger was on Sunday night?'

'She went to a party in London with a woman friend. She told me they caught the 12.20 train back from London, arriving in Oxford at about two in the morning. They got a taxi home from the station. The woman lives next door, actually.' He pointed to the right.

Morse waved to Lewis, who went off to question her.

Morse was already sitting in the car when Lewis joined him ten minutes later.

'He's right. They got back here about half past two in the early hours of Monday morning. That's after the time of the murder, so *she* can't be the murderer.'

'And it can't be Dr Grainger, if he was still in America.' Morse did not seem worried by this.

Lewis was smiling. 'There's something I have to tell you, sir. Yesterday, when we talked to Paul Bayley, he said he'd been with his girlfriend all night.'

'You told me you'd checked his story with her.'

'I did check. Bayley told me that I would find her in the City Library. She was there, and I questioned her. She said her name

90

was Wendy Allworth. She told me she spent the whole of Sunday night with Bayley – they slept on the floor together in a friend's house in South Oxford. But she refused to give the friend's name. Sir, did you see the wedding photograph on Dr Grainger's desk?'

'Yes, but I wasn't close enough to recognize the faces. Was it of Dr and Mrs Grainger?'

'Yes. She's a very beautiful woman, sir – more beautiful than Sheila Poster.'

'I expect she's changed since that picture was taken.'

Lewis gave a happy smile.

'No, she hasn't! You see, I saw her yesterday, in the City Library. "Wendy Allworth" *is* Sylvia Grainger!'

Morse didn't look as surprised as Lewis expected.

Lewis went on: 'And I think it was *Bayley* who was Mrs Grainger's gardener – probably Sheila had told him about the job there – and Bayley fell in love with Mrs Grainger.'

Morse continued the story. 'And Mrs Grainger fell in love with *him*. She told him she wanted to end her marriage, and marry him instead. She knew that her husband and the cleaner were lovers – her husband had told her. But now the cleaner claims she's having a baby. The father's not Grainger, though . . .'

'But Bayley. Yes, sir.'

'And Bayley went to see Sheila on Sunday night – and she refused to do what he wanted – so he murdered her. Is that what you believe?'

'Yes, but how–'

'Tell me, do you think Sylvia Grainger knew about the murder when you talked to her in the library?'

'No, I don't. Bayley probably rang her up after we questioned him, and asked her to tell the police that story – but I don't think he told her about the murder.'

'I agree. She was ready to do a lot to help him, but not that.'

'But sir . . . how do you know all this?'

'Well, this morning I sent a policeman to watch Bayley's house, and to follow him when he went out. At half past one he went to the Randolph Hotel, and met a woman there – a beautiful woman. After he'd left her, I told the policeman to take Bayley back to the police station.'

'So he's there now?' said Lewis slowly.

'Yes, I telephoned them just now. It seems that he's ready to talk. So let's go, shall we?'

Lewis started the car and drove in silence for some minutes. 'Morse has won again!' he thought. Then he said: 'What *did* make you think it was Bayley, sir?'

'A silly little thing, really. When I first saw Bayley, I noticed his hands – short, fat fingers, he has. And then, this morning, I read Sheila's story again – and she talks about the gardener's hands, 'with their short, fat fingers'. But there's another thing, Lewis. So often it's the person who finds the body who was responsible for the murder.'

ACTIVITIES

Three Is a Lucky Number

Before you read

1 Why is it important to be careful about the use of electricity in the bathroom?
2 Find these words in your dictionary:
   bubble   funeral   inspector   will
   Which word discribes:
   a an event after someone's death?
   b something you can find in a soapy bath?
   c a police officer?
   d a document that people write to prepare for their death?

After you read

3 Answer these questions:
   a What was Ronald's reason for marrying Mary, Dorothy and Edyth?
   b Why does Ronald fill the bath with bubbles?
   c What does he expect to happen when he turns on the electricity again?
   d Why does it not happen?
   e What makes Edyth go to the police?
   f What do the police ask Edyth to do?
   g How does she escape from the bathroom?
   h Whose footsteps does Ronald hear at the end of the story?
   i What do you think happens next?
4 Work in pairs. Act out:
   a the first conversation between Ronald and Edyth in the hotel.
   b Edyth's conversation with a police officer after she escapes from the bathroom.

Full Circle

Before you read

5 What qualities and skills does a person need to be a private detective, do you think? Would a man and a woman be equally good at the job?

6 Find these words in your dictionary:

   freeway   lane   lieutenant

   Are these sentences true or false?

   a A freeway is a narrow road for people to walk on.

   b Roads and swimming pools are divided into lanes.

   c Lieutenant is a title for an American police officer.

After you read

7 Match the cars with their drivers. (One drives two cars.)

green Ford	Caroline
Volkswagen	Ron Cagle
small white car	Terry Layton
first blue Toyota	Kinsey Millhone (detective)
second blue Toyota	

8 Who is speaking, who are they talking to, and who or what are they talking about?

   a 'She seems to be alive.'

   b 'They're calling it murder now.'

   c 'The man in the Toyota gave a false name and address.'

   d 'He used to follow her around in a green Ford car.'

   e 'She went her way and I went mine.'

   f 'Somebody stole your plates, and put these in their place.'

9 With a partner, act out a meeting between Lieutenant Dolan and Kinsey Millhone, in which he questions her about the death of the young man in the green Ford.

How's Your Mother?

Before you read

10 How is life in a small village different from city life? What are the advantages and disadvantages of village life, do you think?

11 Find these words in your dictionary:

bury   sergeant

Answer these questions:

a Would you bury somebody *before* or *after* they die?

b Is a sergeant *more important* or *less important* than an inspector.

After you read

12 Answer these questions.

a What does Partridge tell the villagers about his mother?

b How do we find out who really lives in Partridge's house?

c When does he decide to leave his job and go to Canada?

d What makes Sergeant Wallace think that Partridge murdered his mother?

e Why does a woman visit him one cold, dark evening?

f When Partridge goes to the police station to tell his story, Sergeant Wallace does not believe him. Why not?

13 Discuss why Partridge invented a mother. What part did she play in his life?

At the Old Swimming Hole

Before you read

14 Read the first sentence of the story and the questions below. Say what you think.

'I was sitting on a wooden seat at the University of Illinois indoor swimming pool, and I was not enjoying myself.'

a Where is Illinois?

b Why is the woman at the pool?

c Why is she not enjoying herself?

15 Find the word *gamble* in your dictionary. What do *gamblers* do? Explain in your own words.

After you read

16 Number these events in the order in which they actually happened.

..... **A**   Louise is shot.

..... **B**   V. I. is shot in the shoulder.

..... **C**   Alicia is shot.

..... **D**   V. I. visits her old school.

..... **E**   Alicia goes to the school.

..... **F**   Tom and his friend go to the school.

..... **G**   Tom steals Alicia's disks.

..... **H**   Tom borrows a large sum of money.

..... **I**   Tom tells his story to the police.

..... **J**   Alicia tells her story to V. I.

17 Who do you think is the most guilty person in the story? Why?

18 V. I. tries to help her friend. How successful is she?

Slowly, Slowly in the Wind

Before you read

19 Find these words in your dictionary:

corn   scarecrow

Which word describes:

a something you can make?

b something you can grow?

After you read

20 Are these statements true or false? Correct the false ones.

a When her parents separated, Maggie decided to live with her father.

b Skip gave up work because of health problems.

c Frosby wants more money for the fishing rights.

d Skip is very angry when he learns about Maggie's marriage.

e Skip gives Andy a holiday because he wants him to enjoy himself.

f Skip plans the murder carefully.

g Andy is shocked by the murder.

21 Work in pairs. Act out:

    a the first conversation between Skip and Frosby, at Skip's house.

    b the first conversation between Maggie and Pete, at the petrol station.

22 Do you feel sorry for Skip? Why (not)?

Woodrow Wilson's Tie

Before you read

23 Find the word *wax* in your dictionary. What is *wax* made of? What is a *waxwork?*

After you read

24 Choose the correct ending to each statement.

    a Clive's first idea is to spend a night in the Hall of Waxworks

      (i) for an adventure.   (ii) to kill someone.

    b He makes his decision to murder three people

      (i) before his second visit.   (ii) while he is inside the Hall.

    c He puts the bodies in place of the waxworks

      (i) to hide them.   (ii) because it amuses him.

    d When Clive tells the police that he did the murders,

      (i) they don't believe him.   (ii) they put him in prison.

25 Work in pairs. Act out this conversation.

    Student A: You are Clive. Explain to the police doctor how and why you did the murders.

    Student B: You are the police doctor. You do not believe Clive, but he is clearly ill and you want to help him.

The Absence of Emily

Before you read

26 Think about the title of this story. What can you be absent from? What reasons might you have for being absent?

27 Find the word *spade* in your dictionary. What would you use a *spade* for?

After you read

28 Complete the story.
After his first wife [1]..............., Albert marries [2]............... . She has a sister who is [3].............. and [4].............. than she is. While Emily is away at a [5]..............., Albert makes her sister believe that Emily is [6]............... . When Millicent discovers her mistake, Albert agrees not to 7............... . But Millicent has to give him [8].............. .

29 Work in pairs. Act out the meeting between Emily and Millicent after Emily comes home.

The Inside Story

Before you read

30 In this story the murdered woman has written a crime story. How do you think her story might help the police to solve the crime?

31 Find these words in your dictionary. Use them in the sentences below.
clue   earthquake
a The .... caused a lot of damage in Turkey.
b The detectives looked for a .... to help them find the murderer.

After you read

32 Answer these questions.

 a Which two events on the list below come from Sheila's 'inside story'? Cross them out.

   (i)   Sheila writes a story.

   (ii) Morse examines Sheila's body.

   (iii) Dr Grainger goes to California.

   (iv) Lewis's kitchen is repaired.

   (v)   Morse reads Sheila's story.

   (vi) A letter is written with a green pen.

   (vii) A woman is questioned in the Oxford Library.

  (viii) Morse and Lewis talk to Dr Grainger.

   (ix) Bayley meets Mrs Grainger at a hotel.

   (x)   Sheila goes to work for Mrs Grainger.

   (xi) A man and a woman die in a fire.

   (xii) Dr Grainger returns to Oxford from California.

 b Put the other events under the correct headings below, in the order in which they happened.

 Before the story begins   Monday   Tuesday

33 Morse found many clues. Discuss what they were and which one finally led him to the murderer.

Writing

34 Write one of these letters.

  a A letter to Edyth in 'Three Is a Lucky Number' from a middle-aged man who has read about her story in the newspapers. His own wife has died, and he would like to meet her.

  b A report from Kinsey to Mrs Spurrier in 'Full Circle'. Mrs Spurrier already knows who was responsible for her daughter's death. Kinsey is explaining how she found the man.

35 Choose one of these stories. Write a different ending for one of these stories, starting from the line that is given here.

  a ('How's Your Mother?') 'But now I have other things to do.'

  b ('The Absence of Emily') 'What makes you think I *buried* Emily?'

36 Write one of these newspaper reports.

  a ('Slowly, Slowly in the Wind') A report of the discovery of Frosby and Skip's bodies, and the connection between them.

  b ('Woodrow Wilson's Tie') A report of Clive's next crime.

37 Give a short account of how V. I. in 'At the Old Swimming Hole' and Morse in 'The Inside Story' solve their crimes. Include some of the similarities and differences between their cases.

38 Which of the stories do you think is closest to real life?

39 Crime stories usually have a surprise at the end. Which of these stories do you think has the most satisfying suprise?